The Space Between

A PARENT'S GUIDE TO TEENAGE DEVELOPMENT

DR. WALT MUELLER

ZONDERVAN®

ZONDERVAN.com/
AUTHORTRACKER
follow your favorite authors

 youth
specialties

YOUTH SPECIALTIES

The Space Between: A Parent's Guide to Teenage Development
Copyright 2009 by Dr. Walt Mueller

Youth Specialties resources, 1890 Cordell Ct. Ste. 105, El Cajon, CA 92020 are published by Zondervan, 5300 Patterson Ave. SE, Grand Rapids, MI 49530.

ISBN 978-0-310-28771-1

Cover design by SharpSeven Design
Interior design by Brandi Etheredge Design

Printed in the United States of America

09 10 11 12 13 14 • 20 19 18 17 16 15 14 13 12 11 10 9 8 7 6 5

*It's difficult to decide whether growing pains
are something teenagers have—or are.*
—Unknown

*When a child turns twelve you should put him in
a barrel, nail the lid down, and feed him through a
knot hole. When he turns sixteen, plug the hole.*
—Mark Twain

CONTENTS

INTRODUCTION
What's Goin' On?

I WANT TO TELL YOU A TRUE STORY ABOUT ONE OF my sons. Josh, 13, was home alone one summer afternoon when I entered the house without him hearing me. He didn't hear me because he was so totally consumed with consuming the food in our refrigerator.

All I could see were his feet—which weren't moving. The rest of him was hidden behind the refrigerator door. I waited a few seconds to see how much precious electrical energy he intended to waste before I quietly stepped over to where I could get a view of his entire body. Still undetected, I watched with a mixture of horror and pride as my young teenage son held a large plastic jug of chocolate syrup over his head with fully extended arms. With his head tilted back and his mouth wide open, he was squeezing out a thick flow of the sweet stuff with both hands—straight into his mouth.

I cleared my throat to announce my presence. Caught in the act, Josh quickly lowered his head and then spun around to look at me with wide eyes. Because the river of chocolate syrup hadn't shut off before he turned his head, a messy line of it now stretched from his mouth to his left ear.

"What are you doing?!" I asked.

"I'm having a snack." At least he was honest.

I was proud of his resourcefulness. (He wasn't dirtying any dishes.) But I was horrified by what my wife would've thought if she'd seen her son eating like John Belushi's Bluto in *Animal House*.

"Do me a favor," I said. "I'm willing to keep this just between us if you promise to be more human and less animal-like the next time you decide to have a snack. Okay?" He agreed.

Fast-forward two weeks. Here's another true story. Same scene: Josh is home alone. I come into the house undetected. The refrigerator door is standing open, and all I see are his feet, which again aren't moving. I step around the door and catch a view of something even more amazing than his last "snack." His mouth is filled to overflowing with last night's leftover tossed salad. His cheeks are bulging, and lettuce is protruding from his lips. His head is once again tilted back, only now he appears to be impersonating a flower vase. And from the plastic bottle he's holding high above his head, he's squeezing out a river of Italian dressing.

I clear my throat. Josh spins around and chokes a bit when he sees me. Italian dressing now runs across his face the same way chocolate syrup did two weeks ago.

I ask the same question—"What are you doing?!"

After what seems like an eternity of chewing and swallowing, he looks at me with all seriousness and matter-of-factly tells me the truth: "I'm having a salad."

Again, I was both proud and horrified.

Something was happening to my son. He was no longer a little boy; he was growing up. This was the start of a feeding frenzy that would last a few years as he fueled his rapidly changing body and mind. It was also the beginning of more conversations than I'll ever be able to remember during which Josh and I would look at each other in amazement, realizing it was becoming harder and harder to get through to each other, to understand each other. It was the beginning of a time when he'd question our parental wisdom—and often choose to follow a path other than the one we strongly suggested—which usually led to great frustration, disagreement, and conflict.

My son was no longer a dependent child. Josh was on the God-ordained road to becoming an independent adult. And along the way, he was passing through the years of unprecedented change and questioning that we call *adolescence*. I've now watched all four of my kids go through it. If your kids aren't there yet, they will be. And even though I've spent my entire post-adolescent life ministering to, researching, and trying to understand teenagers, every day of my parenting-teens adventure has been full of exciting, and sometimes difficult, surprises.

WHAT'S HAPPENING TO MY KID?
The popular daily comic strip *Zits* offers a hilarious, all-too-true peek into the lives of an angst-ridden adolescent named Jeremy Duncan, his frustrated and clueless parents, and his interesting group of teenage friends. Not a day goes by without Jeremy offering insight into the tumultuous,

change-filled teenage years. And not a day goes by without his bewildered parents looking at each other in confusion, as if to say, "What's happening to our boy?" (Sometimes I imagine the comic strip's creators, Jerry Scott and Jim Borgman, have been living in my house!)

As the parent of four, I've been there—many times over. Parenting teenagers is an important, often joyful journey. But it's not always easy. When you combine raising kids who are confused and sometimes frustrated by the changes going on inside of them (and outside of them) with the normal pressures of our adult lives, it leaves us equally confused and frustrated. Now that I'm on the tail end of it, with just one high schooler left in the house, I can look back and see that just when I was ready to accuse my kids of being clueless, I came face-to-face with the fact that I often had to deal with my own cluelessness.

Some parents dread the teenage years. A father once said to me, "I really love kids, until they're 12. After that, I can't stand them." There was a kernel of truth in this dad's tongue-in-cheek remark as he anticipated his oldest child's 13th birthday. He knew from watching news reports, hearing anecdotal evidence, and observing others raise their kids through the teenage years that there was a good chance life was going to be changing at his house. He was viewing adolescence as something to survive, rather than seeing it as a God-given opportunity to depend on God for guidance and wisdom that would not only help him point his kids to the cross and spiritual maturity, but take him there as well.

LOOKING ON THE BRIGHT SIDE

What comes to mind when you hear the words *teenager* and *parenting* in the same sentence? Over the years I've kept a mental record of parents' responses to this question, and they can be summed up with these words: *Fear, confusion, frustration, misunderstanding,* and *help.* What is it about parenting teenagers that causes us parents to choose these more negative words to describe our experiences and feelings? Why aren't we more positive?

Well, let's face it: Getting kids through the change-filled teenage years can be pretty scary when compared to enduring their childhood years. In addition, teenagers can be very bewildering. One day you're holding your cute little baby in your arms as he coos, cuddles, and looks lovingly into your eyes. (I did that, too.) But before you know it, a major metamorphosis takes place, and suddenly you're reminding your teenager to "look at me while I'm talking to you!" (I also did that.) One father I know likened this transition to the tale of the wolfman. He perceived that his easygoing son had passed through childhood and then simply transformed into a monster one day.

Yes, the unexpected changes that come with adolescence are often shocking, and you may find yourself wondering what's going on. I know I have. And it doesn't take long for bewilderment and confusion to lead to frustration. During childhood your children were fairly predictable. Your parental instincts allowed you to know with some degree of certainty how your kids would respond and react to your comments, direction, and discipline. You more or less knew what would make them happy and sad.

When I was a little boy, my father had a masterful ability to turn my tears and anger into smiles and laughter with a few funny comments or even the dare, "Now, don't you smile!" I was once able to do the same thing with my own kids. Then they entered adolescence, and I began to wonder, *What can I do to get through to these kids?* It was this same frustration that prompted my mother's occasional threats to send me to military school if I didn't shape up. (My own kids would tell you I've pulled that threat out of my bag of lame parenting tricks on more than one occasion.)

Eventually, the confusion and frustration cause some parents to throw up their hands and say, "Would someone please help me understand my teenager?" or "I can't wait for this to pass!" as if the teenage years are a kidney stone.

"NORMAL" ADOLESCENCE?

In the early 20th century, adolescent studies pioneer G. Stanley Hall described adolescence as a period of "storm and stress." Perhaps this is why Sigmund Freud once suggested that adolescence is a temporary mental illness and his daughter, Anna Freud, added, "To be normal during the adolescent period is by itself abnormal."[1] (Can you imagine what it must've been like growing up in *that* house?)

Anne Lamott, one of my favorite writers, relates with humorous, brutal honesty her experience raising her teenage son, Sam:

I thought that there would be a little more downtime. That's a good one. I believed that at some point rather early on, a quiet confidence would inform me, and it did sometimes. But I was stunned by how afraid I felt all the time, too. My friend Ethan says that being a parent means you go through life with the invisible muzzle of a gun held to your head. You may have the greatest joy you ever dreamed of, but you will never again draw an untroubled breath.[2]

Even though my vocational calling and parenting have kept me around teenagers for more than three decades, I'm still working hard to understand them. During all the years I spent working with and observing teens before I became a father, I naively thought I understood them rather well. After all, I was a qualified and professional youth worker. Not only that, but kids weren't running away when they saw me coming. In fact some of them seemed to embrace me more readily than they embraced their own parents. Sure there were things they did and said that were puzzling. But it wasn't until my *own* kids came along and began their teenage journeys that I realized how much I didn't know or understand.

And I'm still learning.

CHAPTER 1
Perspective Needed

MY FRIEND CHAP CLARK SAYS WE'VE COLLECTIVELY struggled in our efforts to describe what an "adolescent" is. While we'd all agree they're human beings living through a life stage filled with tremendous change, we're not sure whether we should look at them as big children or inexperienced adults. I believe this inability to understand adolescence has combined with confusion over our flesh-and-blood kids, creating a mix that leaves young people hurting.

Clark writes,

> This foggy view of the period has given rise to much adult ambivalence and (some would say) systemic neglect. We simply have not agreed on who or what we are dealing with, and it is therefore easier to turn a blind eye to the unique needs of this population.[3]

In my own experience, the blind eyes have too often belonged to parents, teachers, and the church.

We must approach our teenagers with the resolve to never allow our fears, confusion, frustrations, or lack of understanding cause us to turn blind eyes and deaf ears to them. Nor should we expect that as we live through the teenage years, there will never be joy. But as we raise the teenagers we love so much, the changes they experience and the good and bad decisions they make on the road to independence will leave us confused, frustrated, and misunderstood— and that's normal! But our feelings shouldn't prevent us from addressing these realities. Parents should always be asking these questions: *How can I begin to facilitate a smoother adolescent period for my teenager—supporting, loving, and leading my teenager in a way that brings honor and glory to God? How can I begin to break through the walls of confusion, fear, frustration, and misunderstanding? How can I be a positive and proactive bridge-builder into the life and world of my teenager?*

FIRST, A WORD ON ADOLESCENCE

The starting point in this process is to face the truth about who teenagers are and the uniqueness of their life stage. We must constantly seek answers to these questions: *What is their world like? What makes them tick? What changes are they experiencing? What questions are they asking? Why do they think and act the way they do?* And while we ask those questions, we must never forget what Eugene Peterson wrote about this time period: "There are no well-adjusted adolescents. Adolescence is, by definition, maladjustment. And getting adjusted is a strenuous and often noisy process."[4]

In addition we must approach our task of parenting teenagers not as a punishment, a problem, or a cross to bear, but as an opportunity to depend on God while teaching our impressionable teens to do the same.

This process begins with an examination of a simple but fundamental truth about teenagers: *There is a developmental difference between teenagers and adults.* We're at two entirely different stages in the life cycle. Therefore, much of adults' fear, confusion, frustration, and misunderstanding is a normal part of living as a grown-up with a child who's still growing up. In my own life, the difficulty has been increased whenever I've failed to remember that my kids are *not* in the same place that I'm at in life. I've already grown and developed into an adult; but when my children were teenagers, they hadn't yet arrived. Taking the time to understand this fact will help us overcome many of our concerns and close the cultural-generational gap.

Perhaps the relative newness of adolescence being viewed as a distinct period of life and the concept of "teenagers" as we know it today has added to our confusion. While there have always been chronological teenagers (humans aged 13 to 19), teenagers as we know and understand them in our contemporary situation are a relatively new development. There was a time—not long ago—when there were no such things as teenagers or a distinct youth culture.

Believe it or not, it wasn't until 1941 that the term *teenager* was coined and used in, of all places, *Popular Science* magazine. So where did teenagers and today's youth culture come from? Most people don't realize that teenagers as a distinct group are actually a social and economic invention.

In 1930, when the concept of teenagers didn't exist, you simply jumped from functioning as a child to functioning as an adult. At that time, only 50 percent of young people ages 14 to 17 were going to school. The other half were already in the work force.

Then some societal changes took place. An effort was made to get young people out of the work force and into school so they could get an education and so more jobs would be available for family men. When the GIs came home after World War II, America experienced an unprecedented baby boom. This resulted in a growing youth population combined with extraordinary economic growth and opportunity—a mix that left marketers drooling. Lots of children and teenagers with lots of money to spend were too difficult to resist. Those who had something to sell segmented teenagers away from children and adults, creating a distinct youth culture that was targeted with food, clothing, cars, books, movies, and everything else imaginable—all of it made and marketed just for them. By the mid-1950s, teenagers even had their own music (hello, Elvis!) that spoke specifically to their interests and experience.[5]

Unless you've been asleep, you know the rest of the story. Media and marketing have continued to create and reformulate a youth culture that now includes children, teens, and young adults. Because our teenagers are growing through the ever-changing years of adolescence, they're incredibly vulnerable to the youth culture's ability to shape their values, attitudes, and behaviors. And the fact that a growing number of competing messages come at our teens from a variety of directions makes it that much more confusing, frustrating, and difficult for parents of teenagers to understand and connect with their kids. In effect, these changes have made "normal" adolescent development far more complex, added pressures and tensions to the process that never before existed, and widened the cultural-generational gap between teenagers and their parents.

KEEP THESE TRUTHS IN MIND

Before expanding your understanding of adolescent development and the changes your child will face during the teenage years, it's important to understand and embrace several truths. Doing so will provide you with a firm foundation as you grow and live through the adolescent years with your kids. The "storm and stress" of adolescence often leaves parents reeling. I know from my own experience that taking these truths to heart serves as a steadying force. And I believe that if you remind yourself of these things on a regular basis, they'll radically transform your life and the way you approach the valuable years you spend with your teenagers.

Your Teenager Is a Gift from God

We can't buy into the widespread cultural cynicism regarding teenagers and their years of adolescence. It's unjustified. The psalmist writes, "Don't you see that children are God's best gift? The fruit of the womb his generous legacy? Like a warrior's fistful of arrows are the kids of a vigorous youth. Oh, how blessed are you parents, with your quivers full of children!" (Psalm 127:3-5, MSG).

Teenagers aren't liabilities; they're rewards from God given to us as a sign of God's favor. God values them highly and so must we. Because it's so easy for adults to fall prey to the selfish pressures and expectations of life, we can just as easily view teenagers as an inconvenience that sucks the life out of us or a nuisance that keeps us from doing what we want to do and from realizing what we believe is our full potential. When you face difficult times with your kids—and you will—always remember that the children God gave to you as gifts *remain* gifts...even during the teenage years.

Like Everything Else in Life, Parenting Teenagers Isn't Easy

I learned a shocking lesson shortly after the birth of Caitlin, our oldest child, and I've been relearning the lesson ever since: No matter how much time and effort you put into preparing for parenthood, there are always surprises. Some can be devastating and seem paralyzing. Raising and relating to children is difficult work, but it gets more difficult when they enter the adolescent years. And if you have multiple children, then it becomes even more complex as each child has a unique personality and set of life experiences.

Living with and raising adolescents is an experience full of highs and lows. If you're struggling as a parent, don't assume you're alone. You're not. Many of us grew up in and are now living in a church culture in which we do everything we can to keep up appearances. But if the curtain were peeled back and everyone saw the truth about each other and our families, well...we'd all quickly get over the temptation to believe that "my kid" or "my family" is the only one who_____ (fill in the blank with whatever struggle you want).

I've made an effort to be a good parent. I've also made many, many mistakes. At times I've struggled with my self-centered feelings of inadequacy, sometimes falling into the trap of worrying about what other people will think about my shortcomings and my kids' shortcomings. I've grappled with rebellion in my kids. I've known sickening dread, sleepless nights, rage, bitterness, shame, frustration, the disappointment of shattered hopes, and the battle between tenderness and contempt.

If you raise a teenager and are spared all of these experiences, then there are two things you should know. First, you're in the minority. And second, just like all good things in life—it's only by the grace of God. The reality is that parenting adolescents isn't easy. But we can and must approach our role as a glorious, God-given challenge and opportunity. Dr. Paul Tripp reminds us that "the teenage years are often cataclysmic years of conflict, struggle, and grief. They are years of new temptations, of trial and testing. Yet these very struggles, conflicts, trials and tests are what produce such wonderful parental opportunities."[6]

Perfection? There's No Such Thing

As a youth culture analyst, there's one question I get asked more often than any other: "What's the greatest problem facing teenagers today?" My one-word answer is very simple: Sin. It's the same greatest problem facing people of all ages in all times and in all places. It's the same greatest problem I face in my own life. We live in a Genesis 3:6

world. Everything God declared as "good" came undone and is in desperate need of redemption...including us. Each of us has "exchanged the truth of God for a lie" as we worship and serve "created things rather than the Creator" (Romans 1:25).

Anne Lamott sees this so clearly in her relationship with her teenage son. She writes, "It turns out that all kids have this one tiny inbred glitch: they have their own sin, their own stains, their own will. Putting aside for a moment the divine truth of their natures, all of them are wrecked, just like the rest of us."[7]

The root of the problems in our families and homes is the sinful, selfish nature of kids and adults. It can be difficult for us to coexist peacefully. Yes, we must strive to raise spiritually healthy and God-honoring children. And yes, we must never use the reality of human depravity as a reason *not* to pursue godliness and excellence. But it's unrealistic to expect perfect kids, perfect parents, and perfect families. To embrace such expectations is not only bad theology, but it also burdens parents and their kids with never measuring up.

We must never forget that we're all imperfect, flawed, and finite beings polluted by sin, incapable of perfection, and in desperate need of a Savior.

Adolescence Is a Process

Now that three of my four children have moved out of adolescence, I'm realizing that they didn't come equipped with a switch or a button that can be tripped or pushed to either make them accept, embrace, and believe everything I tell them, or to instantaneously morph them into adulthood. Instead, I need to allow them to grow just as I was allowed to grow.

Development is an ongoing process. It doesn't happen instantaneously or overnight. Our role is to consistently model and speak truth into our children's lives as they change and grow. Then we must allow the Holy Spirit to do the work that only the Holy Spirit can do. We serve to guide and direct. God's Spirit works to bring about change and growth at just the right moment—and does so over the course of time. Prayerfully expect God to open your kids' eyes at just the right time—a time that may, in fact, be pretty far down the road.

Independence Is the Goal of Adolescence

I treasure memories of holding each of my four kids for the first time. I treasure memories of watching them change and grow. I can recall thinking intentionally about how difficult it would be to let them go out into the world on their own. I'd look at them, and I couldn't imagine ever being able to let them go.

Now that I'm on the other end of my children's adolescence, I've learned that God prepares more than just our children for independence. God also does something inside of *parents* to prepare us for the moment when we release our children into the world as adults. I can't explain what happens. I just know it does. This, too, is a part of God's plan.

In Genesis 2:24, during a time before sin, God declared that male and female humans will go through a progression in their lives. First, they'll live with their parents. Then they'll leave their parents and cleave to one another in marriage. A slow process of *growing up* and preparing to *go away* takes place. Basically, your children have been designed to become independent adults someday.

Because kids are different, some will reach the goal sooner than others. It seems as though from the moment our daughter Bethany emerged from the womb, she was ready and able to function independently. I can't tell you how many times my offers to help her with homework, college applications, science fair projects, and a whole lot more were met with the same seven-word response: "Dad, I have it all under control."

Adolescent expert Dean Borgman describes the teenage years this way:

> From "Mommy, Daddy, and me," an adolescent must find an autonomous or independent "I." It is not easy, and we adults continually make it more difficult for young people to accomplish. One must be able to see oneself with integrity and clear boundaries, or as a real person, as having a set of values and opinions, and ready to make decisions. To be a healthy and mature man or woman, one must be able to parent oneself (to give self the nurture that once came from parents)...As adolescents we work out our personal identity in contrast to our parents' identity. We push away from that which conceived and nurtured us (Mark 10:7).[8]

Helpless Is a Good Place to Be

Contrary to the opinion that following Jesus is the path to a happy and easy life in which we inherit a pain-free and problem-free existence, the Scriptures speak from beginning to end about the presence and benefits of suffering. We've been conditioned to rely on—among other things—buttons to push and pills to stop the hurt, but the Bible teaches us that suffering and difficulty lead to spiritual growth, a deeper understanding of and dependency on God, and even salvation.

The book of James tells us that we're to "consider it pure joy, my brothers, whenever you face trials of many kinds, because you know that the testing of your faith develops perseverance," which leads us to maturity (James 1:2-4). Many teenagers find adolescence to be a painful and trying time. And as their parents, the teenage years are painful and trying for us as well. However, together with our kids, we can experience the joy of going deeper with God and depending on him during the challenges of adolescence.

The words of Psalm 13 came to have significant meaning for me over the course of several dark and seemingly endless nights. One of my adolescent children had made a series of poor choices. That child's world was shattered, and a steep price was being paid. Feeling as though I'd just been in a train wreck, my mind was filled with questions: *How could this happen? Why did this happen? Have I done anything to cause this? God, what are you trying to teach us? God, do you even care? Will my child survive this?*

I'd heard other parents of teenagers ask questions like these over the years. However, I now realized that you don't really know what it's like until you go through it yourself. And so I spent several nights lying awake in my bed. I spent hours reading the Psalms of Lament as the psalmist asked deep and difficult questions of God—sometimes even shaking his fist at God.

Helpless might be the best word I can use to describe that feeling. If you're anything like me, then you like to be in control. But when it all starts to unravel, life spins around so fast that we don't have a clue what to do. The first part of Psalm 13 records the words of a helpless person who's longing for answers and hope:

How long, O Lord? Will you forget me forever?
How long will you hide your face from me?
How long must I wrestle with my thoughts
and every day have sorrow in my heart?
How long will my enemy triumph over me?
Look on me and answer, O Lord my God.
Give light to my eyes, or I will sleep in death;
my enemy will say, "I have overcome him,"
and my foes will rejoice when I fall.

For several nights my helplessness allowed me to read only these first four verses. It wasn't until a few days later that I began to understand that in the midst of my helplessness, God was seeking to *be* my help. Then I was able to join with the psalmist in celebrating God's goodness through the last two verses of Psalm 13: "But I trust in your unfailing love;

my heart rejoices in your salvation. I will sing to the Lord, for he has been good to me" (vv. 5, 6).

When I look back on the difficult times in my journey as a parent, I sometimes wonder if I could do it all over again, would I choose to change circumstances and events so I'd never experience helplessness? The answer is "No!" You see, in the midst of our helplessness, God reminds us of our need to exercise total dependence on him. God is faithful, promising us the precise measure of grace we need to endure and overcome in times of trial. Suffering and helplessness are redemptive as God does his work in us. In fact, God is in the business of parenting *us* while we're in the midst of parenting the children he's given to us.

Eugene Peterson reminds us that adolescence is a gift from God to middle-aged parents:

Adolescence is not only the process designed by the Creator to bring children to adulthood, it is also designed by the Creator to provide something essential for parents during correspondingly critical years in their lives. Christian parents are most advantageously placed to recognize, appreciate, and receive this gift God so wisely provides.[9]

In his encouraging and vulnerable book *Come Back, Barbara,* Jack Miller recounts years of helpless struggle as a pastor-father whose compliant and seemingly Christian daughter heads off to college and turns her back on her faith. It's a heartbreaking story about his struggle to make sense of Barbara's late-adolescent rebellion, and the difficulty of what was happening in her life. In the end Miller and his wife realized that Barbara was never a follower of Christ in the first place. She'd simply been outwardly compliant without ever having experienced the rebirth of her heart.

Eventually, after years of extreme rebellion against God and her parents, Barbara's life was transformed, she turned to faith, and she reconciled with her father. In hindsight, Miller recognized that Barbara's life wasn't the only one in which God was hard at work. He writes, "So our story comes to its climax with this perception: What seemed to be a tragic defeat for us as parents turned into an unprecedented opportunity to grow and mature as Christians and to learn extraordinary things about God and his ways."[10]

Your teenager will most likely experience difficult times as she goes through the change- and question-filled adolescent years. And chances are you'll be given the gift of difficult times as you live through it with your child. John Foxe, the sixteenth-century English preacher, wrote, "The best teachers are trouble and affliction. These alone give us understanding. How can we feel God's goodness when nothing has troubled us and no danger hangs over our heads?"[11] And Michael Card reminds us:

The path to God is through the wilderness. There, and only there, will we learn what God is truly worth. There we discover His provision: manna, quail, living water. But more significantly, along this path we experience His Presence and discover it is more precious than His provision.[12]

From a human perspective, these are the times when God does his best work in our lives. Our children's growing up is an opportunity for us to grow up—and model what it means to grow up in Christ. If our own helplessness comes through our children's adolescence taking the form of "the wilderness" in our homes, we should embrace it. Suffering is often a necessary step in the process of God refining us and our kids in his image and likeness.

Your Teenager Longs for God

Everyone who's ever walked the face of the earth has been made by God for a relationship with God. Because our rebellion and sin have severed that relationship, there remains a deep yearning inside each human being to have that relationship restored. Blaise Pascal described this universal hole in the soul as a God-shaped vacuum. Alistar McGrath describes Pascal's model as "a God-shaped emptiness within us, which only God can fill. We may try to fill it in other ways and with other things. Yet one of the few certainties of life is that nothing in this world satisfies our longing for something that is ultimately beyond this world."[13]

While at times it may not seem like it, your teenager is no different than anyone else. His great need—whether or not he knows what to call it—is to have this God-shaped emptiness filled by God. If you listen and look closely, you'll see and hear that your teen's music, films, books, magazines, and very life are crying out for spiritual wholeness.

Over the years I've had the privilege of working with thousands of teenagers, and I can't remember one who *hasn't* exhibited this thirst for God. Each of us can look directly into the eyes of the teenagers we know and love and be certain that this, too, is their reality. Even when they don't recognize it as such, we can rest in the assurance that their hunger is for heaven. John Stott reminds us that even when adolescents are running away from God, they know they "have no other resting-place, no other home."[14] This fact should spur us on to constantly and consciously serve as signposts, pointing them to the cross that leads them to their true home.

CHAPTER 2
The Earth Begins to Shake: Understanding Your Developing Teenager

CLINICAL PSYCHOLOGIST EARL WILSON HAS DEFINED an adolescent as "an adult trying to happen."[15] Adolescence is a transitional state; teenagers are neither children nor adults. Everything begins to happen all at once. They look in the mirror and see their bodies changing. The hormonal changes lead to feelings, thoughts, and desires they've never had before. They begin to think about sex...a lot. Friendships and family relationships change. Emotional changes cause them to feel more but understand less. They start to think in new ways. They even begin to question things they always thought were true. Adults tell them they're impulsive, lacking wisdom, and vulnerable to a variety of pressures.

Adolescence is a period full of demands and changes. Peter Zollo, an expert in marketing to teenagers, says emphatically that "teens are not as simple as the one-dimensional portrayals many marketers favor. The teen years are daunting, exciting, and utterly confusing, but rarely ever clear-cut."[16]

The complexity of the teenage years is compounded by the fact that all of these changes occur over a relatively short period of time—at least from our adult perspective. But since a week can seem like an eternity to teenagers, the adolescent years can seem to take forever. I've watched three of my kids grow for 18 years, so I know my perspective is markedly different from theirs. Sometimes a particular stage dragged on for them; but from my perspective, it feels as though I laid them down in their cribs one night, and the next morning I watched them head off to college.

Normal developmental changes cause the dependent child to crave and even fight for adult-like independence and freedom around the age of 11 or 12 (sometimes earlier), leading to six, seven, or even more years of tension and chaos for unprepared parents. With our culture pushing kids to become, act, and look like adults at younger and younger ages, the craving and fighting is starting earlier and earlier.

Again, Anne Lamott puts a smile on my face as she describes her experience:

> Recently I have begun to feel that the boy I loved is gone, and in his place is this male person who pushes my buttons with his moodiness, scorn, and flamboyant laziness. People tell me that the boy will return, but some days that is impossible to imagine. And we were doing so well...I've loved him and given him so much more than I've ever given anyone else, and I'll tell you, a fat lot of good it does these days.[17]

THE TEENAGE TIMELINE

In recent years there's been much discussion among researchers and social observers about the fact that it's becoming increasingly difficult to accurately mark the beginning and end of the adolescent period. David Walsh writes—

> Probably the best way to describe adolescence is to say that it begins at puberty and ends... sometime. That may sound silly and unscientific, but it's the most accurate description of adolescence that I've come across. It is vague precisely because adolescence is an in-between stage determined not so much by what it is but by what it is not. Adolescence is not childhood, and it is not adulthood; it is the period in between those two stages. And because today's kids get through childhood faster than kids did in the past, their transition to adulthood now seems to be taking longer than ever before.[18]

On the one end, an earlier onset of puberty and the fact that kids are dealing with an increasingly complex mix of cultural pressures at younger and younger ages makes them grow up far too fast. Add to that the fact that researchers are finding that more and more young people are acting and living as adolescents beyond their teenage years (also known as "extended adolescence"), and this period of storm and stress for both parents and teenagers is getting longer.

Walsh points out that "in the recent past adolescence began around age thirteen and ended around age seventeen. Today adolescence can last a full fifteen years." [19]

Knowing the ways in which their children will soon be changing can prevent parents from being blindsided. Armed with a working knowledge of normal adolescent development, parents can correctly interpret their children's behavior while helping them through the difficult transition from childhood to adulthood in God-honoring ways. We need to understand why teenagers are so vulnerable. We need to understand that they're in process. We need to recognize that today's cultural forces powerfully shape and mold attitudes, values, and behaviors. By doing so we can change our view of adolescence from negative to positive. We can, as Paul Tripp says, view our children's adolescence as either an "age of opportunity" or a "season for survival." [20] Tripp writes —

> The teen years are often cataclysmic years of conflict, struggle, and grief. They are years of new temptations, of trial and testing. Yet these very struggles, conflicts, trials, and tests are what produce such wonderful parental opportunities. [21]

In my own experience, I've learned to view teenagers — both the ones I've ministered to and the ones I've raised — as those plate-spinning circus performers who used to appear on *The Ed Sullivan Show*. While balancing so many changes and opportunities and influences, teenagers spend their adolescent years struggling to maintain this precarious balancing act. My job as a parent is to seize the God-given opportunity to come alongside my kids, encourage and help them to make good decisions, support them, teach them, pray for them, and help them prioritize their "plates" so they can move through adolescence and on into the independence of a God-glorifying adulthood. In effect, parents are to gradually ease their children into taking ownership of their own lives.

CHAPTER 3
Teenagers Changing Physically

IT HAPPENS SO FAST. THE EVIDENCE IN OUR HOUSE is numerous pencil scribblings on the doorframe of our bedroom. The names, lines, and dates climb higher and higher up the door as markers of our children's growth. On the lower part of the doorframe, the lines are closer together, like the well-spaced rungs of a ladder. These marks remind us of the constant growth of our kids through their preschool and elementary school years. The marks we made during their middle and early high school years sit much farther apart, reminding us of the dramatic growth that took place as they hit puberty.

The God-ordained physical transition from child to adult begins as the body produces and secretes hormones that lead to the onset of puberty. The physical growth and development that follows is rapid. While most kids experience puberty between the ages of 11 and 14, it can occur anywhere from the ages of 10 to 17. In recent years research has found that both boys and girls are entering puberty at younger ages. Back in the nineteenth century, the average age for the onset of puberty was 17. Today, it's happening at an average age of 12.

While no one can be sure why this shift has happened, researchers speculate the change has been prompted by one or more factors, including better nutrition, physiological changes sparked by childhood obesity, an increase in food additives, and the stimulation of hormones prompted by viewing media's growing number of sexually explicit images.[22]

Girls typically enter puberty about 18 months earlier than boys do. Today, the average age for when a girl first menstruates is twelve years and nine months. One hundred years ago, this usually happened two and a half years later—when a girl was 15.[23]

The most notable change for both sexes is the increase in height and weight. When John, a sixth grader, came to our youth group for the first time, the top of his head barely reached my chin. But one look at his feet (several sizes larger than mine), and I knew he was going to be tall. Three years later, this five-footer had grown to be six feet, four inches tall. I realized I'd better start calling him "sir," especially after eating his elbow several times out on the basketball court.

In my own house, Josh's rapid physical development turned our regular father-son wrestling matches—which I'd always won—into one-sided affairs with him as the victor. Two matches that resulted in broken ribs for dad led to my early and sudden retirement from the living room and backyard wrestling arenas. Now I'm smart enough not to even attempt wrestling with my younger son, Nate.

Room Service!

Like other normal teenagers, John and Josh's growth spurts had some side effects. At times they were active and energetic; other times they were lethargic and exhausted. Their sleep was heavy, and their appetites were ravenous. I recently received a powerful visual of adolescent physical development. My son Nate—15 at the time—had joined me on a business trip. But when he opted to skip my "boring" dinner meeting and order room service instead, my last instruction to him had been to "order wisely" (in other words, consider both cost and nutritional factors). When I returned to my hotel room, I opened the door and saw Nate reclining like a Roman Caesar on his queen-sized bed. Surrounded by an array of empty room-service trays and dirty dishes, he was just finishing off a huge plate of ketchup-covered French fries. If I'd walked in any sooner, I'm sure I would have witnessed a typical male-adolescent feeding frenzy.

It's not unusual for parents to notice that their growing teenager is preoccupied, curious, and perhaps even alarmed about the many physical changes taking place. Underarm-hair growth, an increase in perspiration rate, and the appearance of pubic hair are all signs of growing up. And the appearance of acne can be confusing and scary.

Boys will experience the emergence of facial and body hair, a deepening of the voice, a larger neck, muscle development, rapid and dramatic height gain, and a broadening of the shoulders. Girls will become women as they grow taller, their voices lower slightly, their muscles thicken, their breasts develop, their waistlines narrow, and their hips widen.

How Your Teen May React

These normal adolescent physical changes have become even more difficult for our kids to handle due to today's rapidly changing cultural pressures, expectations, and standards for one's physical appearance. You and I went through these same changes once upon a time, and we remember it wasn't easy. But our kids are living in a different world in which the ante's been upped. The media pounds our kids with thousands of images daily, each one contributing to a set of appearance standards that become the benchmark for being normal, acceptable, likeable, and lovable.

As teenagers look in the mirror to monitor where they are in the process, they self-evaluate in stressful ways, determining their physical liabilities and shortcomings based on the standards of beauty portrayed in the multitude of images that have cemented themselves in their mind's eye. They find it extremely difficult to accept who they are in light of who they believe they *should* be.

This desire to achieve to the unrealistic level of societal expectations can lead to a variety of problems, including parent-teen conflicts (over clothing, modesty issues, make-up, hairstyles, body-altering surgical procedures, and so on), abuse of performance- and appearance-enhancing substances, unhealthy obsession with exercise, and even the deadly scourge of disordered eating.

Puberty

There's no question that the most exciting and confusing physical change that occurs during puberty is the body's new ability to produce a child. The external genitals enlarge. Boys begin to produce sperm and have involuntary erections and ejaculations; their penises and testicles grow. Girls begin to ovulate and menstruate. The God-given gift of sexuality takes center stage with all of its newly discovered drives, feelings, and sensations. Boys become men; girls become women. And it all happens so quickly.

Again, our culture offers an extensive, nonstop, confusing mix of messages on how to understand and experience one's developing sexuality. The reality is that voices promoting a biblical sexual ethic and God-glorifying sexual experience (in other words, one that takes place between a man and woman within the covenant of marriage) are increasingly smothered by a barrage of images and messages telling kids that when it comes to sexuality, they can do whatever, wherever, whenever, however, and with whomever...no limits. And increasingly, kids are. Premarital sexual activity, teen pregnancy, out-of-wedlock childbirth, single mothering/fathering, sexually transmitted diseases, oral sex, group sex, and a variety of other social issues are now viewed less as "problems" and more as the accepted norm. One example: MTV and the Kaiser Family Foundation offer kids guidance on how to live out their sexuality via a series of shows and an online booklet under the title, *It's Your (Sex) Life*. The premise is "having sex is a choice and your decision is your own." The only limit is protection of "yourself and your partner." (http://www.kff.org/youthhivstds/upload/MTV_Think_IYSL_Booklet.pdf, p.5.)

This, too, causes a great deal of parent-teen conflict as worldviews and beliefs on sexuality collide.

What You Can Do

Parents can help teenagers through this confusing transition of rapid physical growth by playing the following roles:

Be sensitive and affirming as your teenager's body changes.

Our children need parents who will openly explain and discuss what's happening to their bodies. Our culture constantly sets unrealistic standards regarding physical beauty so that only a handful can measure up. Teenagers spend hours in front of the mirror looking for facial and bodily flaws. Figuratively speaking, they look over their shoulders and see images of the "perfect people"—actors, actresses, supermodels, sports stars, and other media heroes—who "meet" them every day through the Internet, magazines, music, movies, television, and billboards. Our kids have been marinating in these images since the first day they watched television.

Many growing kids believe that a prerequisite for being loved, accepted, and esteemed is to look just like these "perfect people"—and it's painful when they don't. They worry over what the end result of all the changes might be: *Will I be too tall, short, skinny, or fat? Will my* _____ (fill in the name of a body part) *be too big or too small?*

Most of these changes occur during the middle school years, when group acceptance is of the utmost importance and when peers—because of their own impulsivity and insecurities—tend to be the most cruel and insensitive. Life can be miserable for the boy or girl who grows too fast or too slow. A loving and sensitive parent can serve as a buffer in the midst of the type of ridicule that could tarnish a child's self-image. While dealing with these pressures will still be difficult for your child, your positive input will serve to build resiliency into your teenager.

Offer your teenager a godly perspective on these changes.

In addition to modeling the unconditional love and acceptance of Christ during the physically awkward years, Mom and Dad should temper the social pressure of their teenager's outward appearance. Take the time to teach your children about the inward qualities of godliness. Perhaps the best and most powerful lessons will come not from your words but from your example. Be sure your example is void of obsession over your own appearance. It's important to be about the business of developing your own inward character in a godly direction. You, too, are beautiful because of who you are on the inside, not what you look like.

Understand the sexual temptation your teenager faces.

In centuries past (back when puberty arrived at a later age and marriages took place when children were younger), premarital sexual temptation was still present but not as intense. Kids were able to respond to the pressure with some resilience, thanks to a commonly held understanding of sexual parameters, right and wrong, and the expectations of society-at-large. However, the ever-widening gap between the age of sexual maturity and the age of marriage has made it difficult for our kids. Add to that the fact that the newfound and exciting gift of sexuality can be corrupted by a culture that encourages its youngest children to "go for it"—and you can understand why it's very, very difficult for our kids to abstain from sex these days.

So it's crucial that parents understand, teach, and model the biblical perspective of sexuality. In addition, these new cultural realities require parents to speak openly with their children and teenagers about sexuality in age-appropriate ways—even when it makes us uncomfortable. We must live and promote a biblical sexual ethic so our children might experience the God-given gift of sexuality in all of its glorious and enjoyable fullness.

Teach them how to view and treat others with dignity and respect.

Our culture is succeeding at devaluing people to the point at which our kids can be led to believe that others are objects or a means to an end. When it comes to their sexuality, some believe their sexual drives are no different than their hunger for food or thirst for water. Consequently, in their minds food, water, *and* sex all fall into the same category—basic physical needs necessary for survival.

While it might sound crass and crude, the following cultural message of objectification is what our sons and daughters receive daily: *Daughters are taught that they're no different from the porcelain urinals on men's room walls; sons are taught to view females as such—and hey, they can be objectified, too (if they're lucky).* In other words, whenever you get the urge, simply relieve yourself. People have become means to selfish sexual ends. We must go out of our way to address these underlying attitudes and help our kids de-objectify others. God has created *all* people in his image and infused them with dignity.

Communicate openly with your teenager.

It's essential that parents take the time to encourage communication through open discussion with their kids. Not only will you help provide a healthy transition for your teenager, but you'll also reap the benefits of growing family closeness.

CHAPTER 4
Teenagers Changing Socially

MEREDITH'S PARENTS EAGERLY AWAITED HER arrival at the airport. Their oldest child, age 14, had been away at summer camp for an entire month. None of their kids had ever been gone from home for this long. They couldn't wait to spend some uninterrupted time reconnecting with their daughter and hearing all about her camp experience.

The plane arrived. With excitement and a big smile, Meredith ran to the baggage claim area to greet her parents with a big kiss and hug...while she simultaneously texted multiple friends (something she'd done regularly during her time away at camp). The drive to their house was hardly enough time to begin talking. And they hadn't been home for even a few minutes before Meredith was logging onto her computer to check a month's worth of Facebook messages and instant message her friends. Her parents waited patiently in the family room.

After spending about an hour online, Meredith announced that she needed a ride to go see her friend Tracey. And before they knew it, Meredith was gone. Whatever happened to family time?

LEAVING THE NEST

With children from birth to age 10, playmates are important; but when it comes to social networks, home is truly where the heart is. That's not necessarily so with teenagers. Adolescence is a time when teenagers begin to disengage from the family while building extensive and meaningful relationships with their peers. This shift in social orientation from parents to peers is normal. But it can be painful for parents to see their children trade time with family for time with friends.

Some of the time spent with friends takes place outside the home, as kids gather to socialize, shop, or hang out. But today's fast-emerging digital communication technology allows kids to stay in their homes while they separate and disengage from the family in order to network with their peers. All they have to do is log on to their computers to enter into either one-on-one or group chats and instant-messaging sessions. In addition, they can post messages and communicate via any of the many fast-growing Internet-based social networks such as MySpace and Facebook.

Then there's texting. Have you ever observed what happens at the local high school and middle school when the last bell of the day rings? Kids pour out of the doors with packs on their backs and cell phones in their hands. With heads down, they leave school with both hands rapidly typing out text messages—many to friends who may be walking only a few feet away!

As if that's not enough, don't forget game socializing. To wit: I've watched in absolute amazement as my son Nate has not only mastered the world of the Xbox 360, but also hooks up the game platform to the Internet and enters into multiplayer games with others from around the world, using a headset to talk back and forth in real time. He refers to people from around the country and the other side of the globe—whom he's never seen face-to-face—as "my friends." One time I heard him ask a fellow player, "Dude, where are you from?" After a brief moment Nate said matter-of-factly and without surprise, "The Netherlands? I thought I detected an accent."

Dealing with It

And again, while this shift in social orientation from parents to peers is normal, it can be difficult for us parents— especially when the friends they choose are questionable or perhaps totally unknown to us. This is when we must remember that adolescents are on the road to becoming independent adults. They're beginning the process of changing *the nature of their ties*—not breaking ties—with family in order to establish identities of their own. They're developing an increased awareness of the important role that friends play in providing intimacy and emotional support. Neighborhood, school, church, and virtual friends will function as a kind of bridge between the dependence of childhood and the independence of adulthood.

During the teenage years, parents are no longer all-powerful and all-knowing. Your children now see you as you really are—a human being with faults. In fact, they won't hesitate to point out those faults to you whenever they have a chance. The same kids who wanted to take you to first grade show-and-tell now wouldn't be caught dead in public with you.

Several years ago I attended a high school football game on senior night. Before the game began, each senior and his parents were introduced as they walked from the end zone to midfield. Beforehand, the coach had instructed his players to give their moms a kiss when they arrived at the 50-yard line. I'm sure some of them were thinking, *How can he do this to me? How humiliating! Doesn't he know that kissing your mother in public—especially in front of the entire student body—isn't something I want to do?*

It was interesting to watch some of those macho football players kiss their moms in front of bleachers full of their hooting classmates. Because these boys were at varying places in their personal maturity, as well as their relationships with their parents, many found it to be an embarrassing struggle. But others didn't seem bothered by it—they actually embraced the opportunity to honor their moms in this way. While being an adolescent means that you want to build closeness with your friends, at least during this period of life, it might also mean that you don't want to kiss your mother in public.

It's easy for parents to *feel* rejected as their teenagers devote greater amounts of time to building friendships and making social connections, and less time to the family. Don't misinterpret this as rejection. Studies, observation, and discussions with adolescents have all yielded the same result: Parents remain tremendously important and significant in the lives of their teenagers. The everyday evidence may lead you to believe you're being taken for granted, but if you were suddenly removed from the family picture by choice or circumstance, you'd be sorely missed. In fact, a recent survey conducted by the Horatio Alger Institute found that teenagers are increasingly expressing a desire to spend more time with their families.[24]

Perhaps the breakdown of the family in our culture has taken such a toll that more kids are recognizing and appreciating the valuable role that Mom and Dad play in their lives. The good news is that spending time with the family sometimes wins out as a desired activity over spending time with friends, listening to music, surfing the Web, doing homework (not surprising!), and watching TV.

All that said, you can't forget that adolescents are on the road to independence and the nature of your relationship with them will change. But these changes shouldn't be viewed as proof of a deteriorating situation, but rather as a transformation in the *type* of relationship. Be assured that while the nature of the relationship is changing, home is still—in many ways—where their hearts are!

Individuality and Peer Pressure

One interesting aspect of teenage social life is what Teenage Research Unlimited has labeled "indi-filiation." This phenomenon results from the tension between the desire teenagers feel to stand out as individuals (and therefore be cool) and a reluctance to stand out so far that they open themselves up to ridicule and are no longer a part of the group. The term is a "hybrid of two teen need-states, individuality and affiliation" or "shorthand for the way many teens long to stand out from the crowd just enough to be recognized as unique, but not enough to be targeted as a social outcast or even markedly different. To put it in teen-speak, 'I want to be an individual as long as that's what my friends are doing.'"[25]

It's also important to be mindful of the changing nature and role of peer pressure in our teenagers' lives. All of us experienced both positive and negative peer pressure during our teenage years. But peer pressure is different for today's emerging generations due to a variety of cultural shifts. I find it helpful to remind myself of the difference between my experiences with adolescent peer pressure and the peer pressure my kids endure.

When I was growing up, peer pressure typically took the form of a spoken invitation to participate in some sort of behavior that both you and the inviter knew was wrong—due in large part to the fact that there were commonly held standards of right and wrong that we knew we were going to breach. Therefore, we were a bit more covert so as to avoid the consequences. (Remember sneaking a smoke behind the shed?)

But in today's you-decide-for-yourself-what's-right-and-wrong world, peer pressure typically takes the form of an unspoken expectation to participate in behavior that the overwhelming majority of your teen's peers—and our culture—believes is normal, right, and expected. Take a moment to reread those descriptions of peer pressure then and now. Do you see how different and, therefore, more difficult it is for kids in today's world? While we must still teach and model right and wrong, it's important that we do so with sensitivity to the sometimes overwhelming nature of the pressure our kids face.

What You Can Do

There are a number of steps parents can take to help their teenagers transition smoothly through the social development of adolescence.

Remember your role as parents.

From the time they're born, your job is to prepare your children for a lifetime of independence and service to God. You're to love them, train them, *and* let go of them...entrusting them to our heavenly Father along the way.

Don't let your teenager's treatment of you shape how you see yourself.

While teenagers can be incredibly loving and compassionate, they can also be immature, rude, and insensitive. Realize that many of their remarks are a result of the confusion and impulsivity they're experiencing as they change and grow.

Let your teenager know she's loved— no matter what!

The social world of teenagers can be brutal and unforgiving. As teens struggle to find a place to fit in at school, they need to know they're always loved and accepted at home. Parents should continue to provide a secure home base from which teenagers can venture into the stress-filled world of their peers. Studies consistently show that the better a teenager's relationship with her parents, the higher her self-esteem.[26] And "research consistently shows that the most protective factor for teens is parent connection and involvement."[27] Resiliency to negative peer pressure and the ability to take a stand is built into our kids as we give them the ability to fall back on us when it's time to make choices. That resiliency is built *into* our kids through building relationships *with* our kids.

Spend time with your teenager.

If you get so wrapped up in your own life that you fail to invest time in your relationship with your teenager, then he'll look to meet his God-given relational needs in his peer group. Remember: Pulling away from your teenager is like pushing a default button that sends him out of the home to look elsewhere for guidance and direction. If you're frequently absent or too busy, then you forfeit your positive influence.

Look for opportunities to teach your teenager about friendship and treating all people with dignity and respect.

Encourage obedience to the second great commandment—to love our neighbors—by providing a consistent model of that love. Your children should also be challenged to choose friends who allow them to be who God created them to be, not chameleons who have to change colors in order to be accepted.

Encourage your teenager's involvement in friendships with other adults who share your faith and values.

Youth pastors, neighbors, grandparents, a favorite aunt or uncle, and so on, can all serve as listening ears when kids want to talk to someone other than Mom or Dad. When your kids seek out these individuals, don't feel threatened. They can play a valuable role in affirming and cementing the lessons you've already taught your children. Thank God for these significant others.

Never forget that you're still vital.

When my kids were little, they came to me for help with everything from fixing a toy, to assembling a puzzle, to figuring out difficult homework, to learning how to throw and catch a ball. By the time they were teenagers, my unsolicited offers of help were often met with "I can do it myself." Rather than take their desire for more independence as a personal insult or a sign of rejection, I stepped back and simply remained on call and available.

Recently a friend, and the father of three teenagers, asked me, "Do you know when my kids want to talk to me?"

"When?" I asked.

"Whenever they want to." He was learning that you don't necessarily schedule time with your kids as you once did. Instead, you make yourself available at even the most inconvenient times. You must always be ready to take advantage of any relationship-building moments.

Now that three of my kids are beyond the teenage years, they seek my help and advice more freely. I've since realized that even though it didn't always seem like it, I never stopped being an important part of their lives.

Realize that negative peer pressure is a spiritual battle that *all of us*—teenagers and parents alike—fight constantly.

Peer pressure is always there. It's a fact of life in a sinful and fallen world. We may know what's right, and we may even try with all our efforts to do what's right; but we still find ourselves giving in.

The apostle Paul admitted his personal struggle with sinful inclinations:

> My own behaviour baffles me. For I find myself not doing what I really want to do but doing what I really loathe…I often find that I have the will to do good, but not the power…It is an agonising situation, and who on earth can set me free from the clutches of my sinful nature? (Romans 7:15, 18, 24, Phillips).

No doubt Paul would include in this struggle the moral dilemma between deciding to do what everyone else is doing and deciding to do what God says is right and true.

In Matthew 7:13-14, Jesus describes the spiritual struggle of choosing who or what we'll follow in life. He calls us to make the right choice as we stand at a fork in the road. On one side sits a wide gate that opens onto a broad road that's well worn from the number of people who've already traveled it. In fact, many people can be seen walking that way now. But this path leads to death. On the other side is a narrow gate that opens onto a small trail. Maybe we don't see anyone going down that path at the moment, but Jesus still commands us to follow it. It's the path that leads to life.

While Jesus' words were intended to communicate truths about eternal life, eternal death, and what it means to follow him, they also say something about the battle against negative peer pressure. In a sense, our kids often find themselves standing at a similar fork in the road. Some stand there several times a day, in fact, choosing whether to walk the narrow way or travel in the same direction that everyone else is going. It's a dilemma between standing alone as a follower of Christ and going with the flow.

While we need to recognize that our children will make many mistakes and poor choices, we must still point them in the direction of Paul's answer to our human tendency to give in to our sinful nature: "I thank God there is a way out through Jesus Christ our Lord" (Romans 7:25, Phillips).

CHAPTER 5
Teenagers Changing Intellectually

DURING MY OWN ADOLESCENCE, PART OF MY world shattered when I realized that while I was the one growing up, *my parents were the ones who were changing*. No longer were they intelligent...or at least, that's what I thought. To be honest, this reality rocked my world. I'd always looked up to my father as the smartest man in the world, but suddenly he seemed to be ignorant toward many of the issues I was facing in my young teenage life. I began to wonder how my parents had survived for so long in the big, cruel world when they were so...out of touch and uninformed!

I remember numerous family dinner conversations about politics, religion, current events, sports, relationships, and a host of other topics. My father would offer his insights while my younger brothers would soak it all in. They seemed to believe every word he said without question. As an older and more knowledgeable teenager, I felt it was my responsibility to challenge my father's inferior, off-base way of thinking. After all, I was now able to understand things I'd never been able to understand before. And of course there was my youthful idealism, which led me to criticize anyone who *didn't* share my opinions and ideas.

My distrust of adults' opinions and intellectual capacity extended to the halls and classrooms of my high school. My peers and I viewed our teachers as being somewhat knowledgeable in the fields they taught. (We had to—they controlled the red pen.) But when talking about life, instead of math or English, the teachers were just as ill-informed as our parents. We teenagers had it all figured out.

I guess what goes around comes around. When my son Josh was about five years old, he and I were driving in the car. After looking out the back window at the setting sun, he leaned up and looked into the eastern sky to see the moon.

After another look back at the sun and a look ahead at the moon, he turned to me and asked, "Hey, Dad, how come when the sun is still out the moon is up, too?"

Good question. After thinking a bit, I explained that God made the world so there would always be a light to shine, one during the day, and one during the night. Then I stepped down to his level and said, "And he made it so that when Mr. Sun is ready to go to bed, Mr. Moon is already up and ready to take over."

After casting a couple more curious glances at the sun and the moon, my little boy turned to me and said adoringly, "Man, Dad...you know everything!"

And then he grew up and turned into a teenager. Suddenly, I knew a lot less.

"WHAT'S GOING IN THAT HEAD OF YOURS?"

What was happening to me when I was a teenager? And in the same way, why did Josh's perspective on my intellectual capabilities do an about-face when he became a teenager? As parents we can understand some of our teenagers' intellectual changes by looking at the work of Swiss psychologist Jean Piaget, who pioneered some of the most significant research in the area of child and adolescent intellectual development. Piaget found that young children pass through four distinct intellectual stages by the time they reach the age of 11 or 12.

- First, the *sensorimotor stage* (from roughly birth to two years) when a child's intelligence is manifested through actions. Every parent remembers the joy of watching their child progress from acting solely on reflex to using their senses to solve problems like reaching for a toy or opening a door.

- Second, the *preoperational stage* (from roughly two to seven years) when a child has the capacity to use language and play make-believe. The developing child uses her imagination, for example, to pretend that a block of wood is a car or that two sticks held together is an airplane.

- Third, the *concrete operations stage* (from roughly seven to eleven years). The child is now able to use limited logic to solve simple problems. Children in this stage see things literally and think in terms of facts. They see social problems and issues in terms of black and white, right and wrong.

The intellectual abilities of children are limited. Mom and Dad, along with most other adults, are viewed as being knowledgeable and correct on most matters. This makes life around the house fairly stable and comfortable. But things change when a child enters adolescence. They certainly did for me when I was a teenager. In hindsight I realize that my parents hadn't changed; I had.

Although I didn't know it at the time, adolescence had ushered me into Piaget's fourth stage: *Formal operations* (from roughly 12 to 15 years). I now had the ability to use more advanced logic to explore and solve complex hypothetical problems about the world on my own and assess the possible consequences of different courses of action. My brain was maturing along with the rest of my body, and I was becoming an adult in terms of my ability to think. I hadn't "arrived" by any stretch of the imagination (I didn't know this at the time, though), but I was on my way.

IT ALL ADDS UP

Recent developments in the area of brain research are especially encouraging for parents of teenagers. This research points to the wonder and complexity of how God made us, as well as the God-ordained process of human growth and development. In years past it was assumed that a child's brain was fully formed somewhere between the ages of eight and twelve. But new research and scientific advances—along with the use of magnetic resonance imaging (MRI) technologies—show that the brain is an organ that grows and transitions, just like the adolescent. Not only does the brain go through a period of growth during the time between puberty and young adulthood, but the brain's hardware and software also go through a process of "wiring" or "pruning."

The brain's limbic system is the area deep within the brain that generates emotions, including rage and fear. With hormones surging during adolescence, the limbic system is affected in ways that can intensify aggressive emotions, particularly in boys. Research shows that the brain's prefrontal cortex is the last part to develop. This is the area that controls impulses, planning, organizing, prioritizing, judging future consequences, making complex assessments, self-control, and emotional regulation.

Laurence Steinberg, an expert on brain development at Temple University, says,

> The parts of the brain responsible for things like sensation seeking are getting turned on in big ways around the time of puberty, but the parts for exercising judgment are still maturing throughout the course of adolescence. So you've got this time gap between when things impel kids toward taking risks in early adolescence, and when things that allow people to think before they act come online. It's like turning on the engine of a car without a skilled driver at the wheel.[28]

When all is said and done, the research shows that the brain may not be fully formed until the age of 24 or 25.

This groundbreaking research explains a lot about teen

behavior. Teenagers have difficulty controlling their impulses, they lack foresight and judgment, and they're especially vulnerable to peer pressure, which may explain why they're more prone than adults to shoplift, smoke, experiment with drugs and alcohol, not use seat belts, and engage in a host of other risk-taking behaviors. Their growing and developing brains can also sustain severe immediate and long-term damage when alcohol and other illicit drugs are introduced into their systems. Without knowing it, many teenagers are damaging and altering the wiring and synapses in their brains—for life.

THE TEENAGE BRAIN AND SEXUALITY

Now consider what this new research has discovered about the damage and alteration that occurs in the brain as a result of premarital sexual activity. Drs. Joe S. McIlhaney, Jr. and Freda McKissic Bush from the Medical Institute for Sexual Health offer compelling information and advice related to adolescent brain development and teen sexuality in their book *Hooked: New Science on How Casual Sex Is Affecting Our Children*. The irony is that while cultural sexual pressures will combine with teenagers' intellectual immaturity and sinful natures to lead them to compromise their sexuality before marriage, damage to their brains can affect the ways they're able to relate to others and experience their sexuality in God-honoring ways for the rest of their lives.

McIlhaney and Bush report that premarital sexual activity can damage "the important, built-in ability to develop significant and meaningful connection to other human beings. Another negative consequence is that as young people experience these sexual relationships" it's "molding them to not only damage their attachment ability but to become desensitized to the risk of short-term sexual relationships, eventually believing that this behavior is harmless and acceptable, and does not involve the psychological and mental health part of themselves."[29]

On the other hand, research is showing that a healthy and God-honoring sexual relationship "strengthens the brain cell connections associated with 'attachment' of one person to another, helping to ensure the permanence of the relationship that finds its healthiest expression with sexual consummation in marriage."[30]

Generally speaking, McIlhaney and Bush advise parents to realize that "while young people can make some good judgment calls for themselves, it is impossible for them to make fully mature judgment decisions until their mid-twenties, when their brains are fully mature."[31] The implications are clear: Our kids need us to consistently model and teach a biblical understanding of their God-given sexuality. We can't stand back in silence.

It's amazing, but maybe not too surprising, to realize that even our brain makeup and chemistry point to the fact that God made us to be integrated selves. In other words, the decisions we make have consequences for all areas of our lives. For teenagers, all of whom are still developing intellectually, this means their bad decisions—which, in part, flow from undeveloped and impulsive brains—can impede the healthy and proper development of their brains.

I often recall my own teenage years and some of the impulsive decisions that led to my saying or doing things that I quickly regretted. My dad would often question the root of my impulsive behaviors by asking that oft-repeated fatherly question, "What in the world were you thinking?" I've asked the same question of my own kids, and their answers echo mine at that age: "I don't know." (Really, I didn't.) Since then I've come to understand that if you believe teenagers are clueless as to why they do the things they do, there are times when that might be true.

What You Can Do

As parents, encourage the use of these new intellectual capacities by doing the following:

Discipline yourself.

While there may be marked differences in the ways teenagers view the intellectual capabilities of adults, their newfound and developing ability to reason as adults will make for some interesting conversations and confrontations at home. Sometimes the best approach is for parents to bite their tongues, understanding that this is a part of normal adolescent development, and that it's better—as the author of Proverbs writes—to listen before giving an answer (Proverbs 18:13). Remember, your adolescent is not an adult. Therefore, you can expect a mix of developing and not-yet-there adult thinking ability tainted by immaturity, impulsivity, and inconsistent logic. As Raymond Duncan once said, "The best substitute for experience is being sixteen!"

Think with, not for.

Wise parents learn that while it's important to continue to offer structure, guidance, direction, advice, and explanations to their offspring, they should also give their children some freedom to make their own decisions. Some of the best lessons are learned through discovery. Your kids will appreciate this, and it will benefit them in the long run. Parents who continue to do all the thinking for their teenagers will raise adults who have difficulty making vocational, marriage, educational, time management, ethical, and other important choices.

In our family the general rule has been this: *When they're children, we think for them. As they move into adolescence, we think with them, tempering their decisions by modeling and talking about choices that bring honor and glory to God. We do this so that when they become adults, they'll be able to think for themselves in responsible, God-honoring ways.*

Challenge your teenager to reflect on issues about which you might not see eye-to-eye.

By doing so you'll model and encourage responsible critical thinking. One area where most of us knock heads with our kids is their media choices (i.e., music, movies, gaming, TV, radio, Internet). But instead of "thinking for them" by enforcing parameters with no reason beyond "because I said so," why not embrace your differences as an opportunity create discussion, challenging them to think critically on their own? In our house I don't hesitate to verbalize my concerns regarding media themes and content. Still, I invite my kids to make a case for why I might be wrong. At times, I am wrong. But I always view and listen with them, then offer my opinion, working to communicate how I've come to those conclusions. (I created a media evaluation paradigm for this purpose called *How to Use Your Head to Guard Your Heart: A 3(D) Guide to Making Responsible Media Choices*—read more about it at the Center for Parent/Youth Understanding Web site: www.cpyu.org).

Encourage discussion and be sure to listen before offering advice.

Teenagers who sense they've been respected and heard are much more prone to listen to those who've first listened to them.

Treat your teenagers as adults.

Not just any adults, though. Treat them as adults whose opinions you value by allowing them an increased role in the family's decision-making process.

Always teach right and wrong and be sure to explain and enforce appropriate consequences for wrongdoing.

In effect, you'll become your teenager's prefrontal cortex. You'll provide the structure that's lacking in adolescents' developing brains. There are times when we have to protect our children from themselves.

WHAT GOES AROUND, COMES AROUND

When I was 15, my parents allowed me to purchase a $25 car. (Remember those days?) Believe it or not, the thing ran even though it needed some major work. I spent hours driving it up and down the driveway and tinkering under the hood in preparation for the day I'd turn 16 and could take it on the open road. Shortly after purchasing the car, I decided it was time to replace the muffler. I grabbed my toolbox, crawled under the car, and began working to remove that old muffler. It was so rusted that it wouldn't budge, and I spent the entire day pounding with a hammer.

Sensing my frustration, my dad appeared from time to time, leaned under the car, and asked if I wanted his help. Each of his inquiries strengthened my adolescent determination and resolve to do it myself. As the day came to an end, he appeared one last time. He suggested that I was hitting the muffler in the wrong place. (This seemed absurd since I'd already pounded on every square inch of the crazy thing.) He went on to say that if I'd only let him take a shot, he knew he could get it. That made me more determined than ever to show him that I was right and I could do it. What did he know, anyway? It was shaping up to be one of those great father-son showdowns.

The next day I angrily went back to work. Several more frustrating hours passed. And soon I was steamed at not only the muffler that wouldn't budge, but also my dad who kept making those irritating appearances to offer his expertise.

I finally gave in and agreed to let him take a look, hoping that when he crawled under that car, he'd be pounding away for several hours. Dad asked me to hand him my hammer, and then I stood there and waited, knowing I was right. I heard him take a swing or two with the hammer, and then I heard the most terrible noise I'd ever heard in my life—the sound of that rusty muffler hitting the driveway. I was so angry! I couldn't even bring myself to tell Dad that I'd most likely loosened the thing for him.

As my dad slid out from under the car, he didn't say a word. He just smiled from ear to ear. I looked at his smug expression and shouted, "Why do you always have to be right?!" From that moment on, I tried to forget what happened. And to this day, my dad continues to tell this story—with that same ear-to-ear smile on his face.

Years later, when I was a college student, an amazing thing happened. As I sat talking to my parents during a holiday break, it dawned on me: They were no longer stupid! This seemed strange since I was the one who'd gone off to college. But my parents were now smart again. I'd matured and honed my intellectual capacities enough to see that they were actually pretty wise. I was no longer young enough to know everything! I'm not sure if it was that day or sometime shortly thereafter, but I told my parents how I'd regained my respect for them and their wisdom.

My dad simply responded, "Remember the muffler!"

A few more years later, I'd get stupid again—at least that's what my teenage kids believed. But now they're getting older, and suddenly, I'm getting smart again. What goes around comes around. If you're struggling with an intellectually superior teenager, trust me, there will be a day when you, too, will get smart again.

CHAPTER 6
Teenagers Changing Emotionally

MOST PARENTS WOULD SAY THEY EXPERIENCED the easiest and most crisis-free years of parenting when their children were young. That's certainly been the case in our house. If children are raised in a loving home absent of stress-causing turmoil (death, divorce, abuse, chronic illness, and so forth), then their emotions will usually be stable and predictable.

The emotional stability of most children parallels the stability of childhood in general. If our children's days are filled with play, a routine school life, and relatively little pressure, then they can remain on an emotionally even keel. Rarely is the boat rocked in major ways. A high school student once told me, "I wish I could go back and be a fourth-grader again. Life is so easy when you spend your days playing and riding your bike. I was always happy."

As parents we know what makes young children happy or sad. When a child is angry, upset, or crying, a parent can find ways to calm and comfort the child rather quickly. Tears can turn to smiles in a matter of seconds. Children find it easy to forgive, forget, and move on like nothing ever happened.

Now contrast childhood with the words I once heard from a 16-year-old girl: "I never in my life want to go back and be an adolescent. I want so bad to get it over with." As life gets harder and more complex for teenagers, the normal developmental issues they face are compounded by cultural pressures and relational breakdowns that make it that much harder.

THE STRESS TEST

Imagine what we might discover if we were to administer one of those written "stress tests" to the typical teenager. Perhaps you've seen them or even taken one yourself. Designed to measure the amount of stress an adult is experiencing, the test is based on strong scientific evidence that the greater the number of "social readjustments" that individuals must make, the greater their chances of experiencing significant physical and emotional health problems.

The test lists 65 changes and milestones—ranging from death of a spouse to geographic relocation to change in financial status to holiday travel—that people may experience. Each of these changes is assigned a point value based on the severity of the event. By marking those changes and milestones experienced in the last 12 months and then totaling the number of points assigned to each one, a person receives a picture of the amount of stress they're currently under.

It would be fairly easy to list 65 stress-causing changes associated with normal adolescent growth: Physical growth, new sexual urges, changing relationships, cultural pressures, and the desire to be accepted, just to name a few. All "normal" teens would be hard-pressed not to circle every one of them. But along with this flood of changes, adolescents must face the real possibility of physical and emotional difficulties. Add to that the fact that many teenagers live with divorced parents and blended families and the stress levels rise even more.

THE EARTHQUAKE OF ADOLESCENCE

I've found it helpful to visualize the teenage years as "the earthquake of adolescence": They arrive swiftly, pass quickly, and leave the landscape of a child's life radically altered. If we could put a face on the toll of the stress that occurs during the teenage years, it might resemble the faces shown during news footage of earthquake victims.

I have vivid memories of the Loma Prieta earthquake that struck the San Francisco Bay Area on October 17, 1989. I was watching the pre-game show for a World Series game between the San Francisco Giants and the Oakland As. A commentator on the field looked around in confusion as the earth began to shake. Then the TV signal was lost. When the picture finally returned, baseball was the last thing on anyone's mind. Cameras took us throughout the Bay Area just minutes after the quake ended, and live pictures showed dozens of panicked people near crumbled buildings. Some cried. Some stood dazed. Others comforted neighbors they'd never met before. Still others wandered the streets, struggling to comprehend what had happened and often without a clue as to what to do next.

To me, these images looked an awful lot like the ways kids respond to the tumultuous years of adolescence. For some it's devastating. Others weather the shifts with relative ease. What are the normal emotional changes you can expect when the earthquake of adolescence shakes the foundation of your home? Well, sometimes you don't know what to expect. Mood swings from the highest of highs to the lowest of lows can occur suddenly and then end just as quickly—or they can last for several days (aftershocks included).

Many of these mood swings are directly related to the physical and social changes taking place. A glance in the mirror can trigger a quick drop on the steepest hill of the roller coaster of adolescent emotions. Self-criticism of what your teenager sees, or what she thinks her friends see, can lead to feelings of loneliness and worthlessness. Being an early or late developer has repercussions on a teenager's emotional well-being in a society that's preoccupied with appearance. Negative mood swings can also result from academic failure, poor peer relationships, family disunity, a break up, and the anxiety of perceived rejection by members of the opposite sex.

Periods of elation, excitement, and youthful exuberance are triggered in numerous ways, too. A young teenage girl gets a text message from an interested boy. She's up! In fact, she's so up that nobody in the world, but especially Mom and Dad, can understand the depth of the love she's feeling for this special guy. Climbs up the roller coaster can also result from peer acceptance, the purchase of a coveted object, academic success, making the team, and other achievements.

TEENS' SPIRITUALITY MAY BE VOLATILE, TOO

It's important to note that adolescent spirituality can also be full of ups and downs. Because of where they are developmentally, teenagers' faith will tend to be more informed by their feelings than the factual certainty of God's character and love as described in his unchanging Word. Add to that the fact that they're growing up in a postmodern world that tends to embrace feelings over fact, and kids are likely to alternate between feeling good about their faith because they feel close to God and feeling down about their faith because they aren't feeling God's presence.

In addition, be aware that your teenager may embrace a faith and a "god" defined more by their feelings than by fact. The postmodern world has rejected modernism's rationality and reason, and it plays well to developmentally vulnerable kids. Kids choose to believe and live by "what I like" or "what feels good to me." Ravi Zacharias says the postmodern generation "hears with its eyes and thinks with its feelings."[32] Consequently, more and more of our kids construct their own spiritual reality and beliefs using personal, subjective experience as their authority.

What You Can Do

The bottom line is that when it comes to teenagers and their changing emotions, strange behavior is often normal. But don't ever forget that parents play an important role in helping teenagers understand and handle their emotions in healthy ways. Here are a few suggestions on how to offer stability when those topsy-turvy teenage emotions seem to be out of control.

Treat your teenagers' emotions as important.

I know you'll be tempted—I've been there—but don't ever become insensitive. A teenager's emotions are very real to him. Many feelings stem from a preoccupation with self and the accompanying fear of rejection. Teens expect their parents will always love and accept them. To be written off by an insensitive parent is the type of rejection that can send a "normal" teenager over the edge to clinical depression and even suicide. Much of a teenager's emotional resilience is built in and through a healthy relationship with Mom and Dad. What teens need are parents who will hang in there and love them despite the emotional ups and downs over what may seem to be trivial things. Remember, what's little to you might in fact be very big to him. Even when we're convinced our kids are overreacting (and they probably are), they're just handling their confusion in the best way they know how. Listen sensitively as they share their joys and fears.

Make every effort to ensure that your home is emotionally stable and secure.

Our rapidly changing culture often gives kids a world that is ugly, full of rejection, confusing, and unforgiving. The home must continue to be a shelter and fortress marked by unconditional acceptance and love. If you and your family aren't moving in that direction, secure the assistance of a Christian family counselor.

Look for and emphasize your child's positive qualities.

Your teenager's peer group, especially if your child is in middle school, can be brutal. Peers can create, find, and point out all kinds of negative things in a way that verges on harassment. You can balance that negative influence by encouraging your teen in the abilities and activities where she does well. Over the years I've asked lots of teenagers what makes them happiest in life. They consistently tell me they're happiest when their parents say, "I love you" or "I'm proud of you." Have you said these things to your teenager lately?

Don't take your teenager's rejection personally.

Expect that some of your encouraging advice might be rejected. Don't base your mood, self-acceptance, or understanding of your own parental effectiveness on how your kids feel about you or treat you. Your role is to consistently love and encourage your child while finding your identity in Christ alone.

Ask questions if your teenager's moods are often low—really low.

Sometimes we can fall into the habit of blaming all negative or moody behavior on normal adolescent development. But there are times when the negative moods are a sign of a more severe and lasting issue or a combination of problems that have led to depression. Don't be afraid to probe (and do so in specific, thoughtful ways) if you suspect that something more significant is going on beneath the surface.

Always, always, *always* emphasize the authority of the Word.

Most teenagers don't realize that all of the decisions they

make in life are based on some authority. Usually it's a combination of authorities they've adopted unconsciously, including peers, media, parents, self, and so on. While it's worth seeking out and accepting wise advice from these people and things, the primary authority we're called to consciously live under is the authority of the One who made us. We must teach our students to recognize, understand, and embrace God as the Authority in their lives. They must look to the incarnate Word Jesus who said in Matthew 28:18, "All authority in heaven and on earth has been given to me," and to God's revelation in Scripture, which is "God-breathed and is useful for teaching, rebuking, correcting and training in righteousness" (2 Timothy 3:16), to guide every step of their lives.

Teach your children to trust truth over feelings.

But don't stop there. Teach them how the authoritative Word speaks to every area of life, going to great lengths to speak God's truth on matters to which they're deferring to the authority of their feelings. In our postmodern world, we can easily be tempted into *feeling* as though we should downplay any truth claims, including those found in Scripture. It would be a shame for history to remember our era of parenting as the watershed moment when dads and moms didn't do enough to help their kids embrace the authority of the Word over the whims of their own windblown emotions. Feelings should never eclipse truth. Truth should always direct our understanding of our feelings—the only trustworthy feelings are those grounded in truth.

I recently had a discussion with a college graduate about a major decision she'd made. I didn't know her well, but she asked for my opinion. Before voicing my concern about what I saw as an obvious disconnect between her professed faith and her choice, I wanted to know more about how she came to make her decision. She summed it up in four words: "It just felt right."

When I was a teenager, my dad noticed that I had a bent for making impulsive decisions based on my emotions. He warned me that my feelings could play tricks on me; that they were unreliable; and that if trusted, they could lead me down the path of making many unwise, dangerous, or even immoral choices. I'm not sure he "felt" I was listening at the time, but his warnings did sink in—albeit slowly. In fact, it took some hard lessons learned—the results of my feeling-oriented choices—to help me see just how tricky emotions can be.

I've learned to avoid making important decisions when my emotions are especially high or especially low. If I don't, then I might give my feelings the sway they shouldn't have. Walk your teenager through the Scriptures so he can see how fickle emotions can be. The Old and New Testaments are full of examples of people who allowed their feelings to eclipse the truth and later suffered the consequences for it. (For example, David and Bathsheba, Lot's wife, Ananias and Sapphira, and so on.) The Bible and the history of the Church are also filled with stories about people who refused to equate the absence of good feelings with the absence of God (Noah, Abraham, Joseph, David, Job, Paul, and so forth). They held onto the truth they knew, even though their feelings and circumstances tempted them to do otherwise. One of the best and most convincing tools in your parenting arsenal is to become vulnerable with your kids, sharing the good, bad, and ugly from your own life and feeling-based choices.

Make sure your children know that following Jesus doesn't always feel good.

I have many fond memories of a childhood spent in Sunday school. Our teachers utilized all the high-tech tools of music, puppets, crafts, and flannelgraphs. What I remember the most is the music, particularly the songs still ingrained in my mind, due to weekly repetition. But over the years I've come to regret remembering a few of those songs because they were filled with lies and bad theology. I believe some songs actually did more harm than good.

Do you remember singing, "Happy, happy, happy, happy, happy are the people whose God is the Lord"? I do. It messed me up. For a long time, I believed that difficulty was a sign of the absence of God's blessing and presence in my life. It wasn't until later that the words of Jesus in Matthew 16:24—"If anyone would come after me, he must deny himself and take up his cross and follow me"—suddenly became real as I finally understood that discipleship is costly, painful, and usually quite difficult. Martyrs for the faith know God's grace, mercy, and peace; but I don't believe they feel "happy" or good—physically or emotionally—while dying for their faith.

Chances are your kids won't be martyred. But they'll suffer in this life. Many teenagers are suffering already. They need to know that growth usually comes through suffering. In the words of one preacher, "God often puts his children to bed in the dark." We rarely like or enjoy suffering. So we need to teach our kids to meet the unchanging God who is—rather than invent a god that makes sense at the moment—in the midst of their suffering.

Give your children the knowledge and skill to utilize the "this I knows."

My wife teaches three-year-olds in Sunday school. Over the course of the year, she leads them through the memorization of eight questions from the Children's Catechism. She asks the questions, and they recite the answers back to her... week, after week, after week. In our worship service, we recite the Apostles' Creed...week, after week, after week. Some might believe we're subjecting ourselves to brainwashing or, at the very least, meaningless empty ritual. But this has become one of the most valuable moments of my week. And I pray it would be the same for the kids.

During the week, I face challenges to my faith—some of them are quite attractive and compelling. Emotionally, I might even want to "go for it." But then I remind myself of the "this I knows"—truths that never waver or change—which keep my emotions, and the dangerous choices that could result from trusting them, in check. I've learned to talk to myself rather than listen to my emotions. We'd serve our kids better if we filled their wells full of "this I knows."

The emotional earthquake of adolescence doesn't last forever. Kids whose parents help them rebuild on the foundation of a loving and accepting family are more likely to move into a strong and healthy adulthood with thankfulness for a dad and a mom who understood and cared when the going was especially rough.

CHAPTER 7
Teenagers Changing Morally and Spiritually

CHRIS WAS RAISED IN A CHRISTIAN HOME. HIS parents deliberately and consistently nurtured his faith in Christ from the time he was born. A star pupil in Sunday school, he couldn't stand to miss a week. He grew up with a well-deserved reputation for having mastered the facts of the faith. But Chris knew even more than facts and figures since he'd dedicated his life to loving and serving Jesus Christ at a young age.

As Chris entered the teenage years, his parents and youth leader began to notice a change in his attitude. Chris was becoming skeptical about the most basic facts and tenets of the faith he'd so readily embraced before. Gradually, his interest in spiritual things appeared to fade as he became more involved in sports. Before long, he was dating a girl who wasn't interested in his church or his faith. He began to question the existence of God, the reliability of the Bible, and everything that—in his words—he'd "blindly" and "naively" believed.

What happened to Chris? Children from birth to age 10 have a blind-faith tendency to accept without question the values and beliefs of their parents. While they don't have a deep knowledge of biblical facts and theological truth, they do believe in what Mom and Dad taught them (which is often reinforced at church). But it won't necessarily stay that way during adolescence. Armed with a newfound ability to think, evaluate, and solve problems, teenagers often question the values and beliefs they'd previously accepted. They'll take what you've handed down to them and put it to the test.

TELL THEM ABOUT JESUS...BUT LET THEM QUESTION THEIR FAITH

In today's postmodern world in which the culture (and many teenagers) wears spirituality on its sleeve, your children will encounter a variety of spiritual options, faith systems, and combinations thereof that seem quite appealing. In addition, our culture's emphasis on pluralism, diversity, and tolerance has created an environment in which different spiritualities aren't seen as mutually exclusive. In fact, our culture sees it as being wise and broad-minded to embrace and combine elements of different spiritualities into your own personal belief system.

Parents and youth workers should certainly tell the truth and point kids to the truth. But we must also take courage, realizing that when teenagers question the Christian faith while investigating other faith systems, they may in fact be taking steps toward *a vital faith in Christ*. What you believe indicates a weakening or disappearing faith in God might be the very thing God uses to reinforce, cement, and strengthen their faith as it passes through the Refiner's fire of speculation, examination, doubt, and questioning. As Eugene Peterson reminds us, "Adolescents are nothing if not spiritual. Spirituality emerges in adolescence with a vengeance."[33]

These realities require us to love and minister to our kids with fortitude, diligence, and grace. Chap Clark says,

> One of the most significant changes I have observed over the past three decades is how much longer it takes for faith to be rooted in a young person's life. Internalizing and personally owning faith in a way that guides and shapes a life often takes years. Veteran youth workers have a nagging feeling that this laborious journey to faith is universal, even among adolescents from spiritually supportive family systems...The process of helping an adolescent develop a consistent faith takes time, patience, and perseverance. Faith is a long, complex journey, and adolescents need someone who will walk alongside them as long as it takes.[34]

Fortunately, nobody ever wrote Chris off as a hopeless spiritual rebel. His parents and youth worker allowed him to think for himself and openly discussed his questions while challenging his changing values and behaviors with the truth. They understood that his developing intellectual capacity was leading him to think more deeply about theological concepts. They prayed hard. They continued to love him. They continued to live out their faith before Chris as they confidently walked in the presence of God. Sure, it was difficult for them. But by reminding themselves of God's sovereignty and what was *really* happening beneath the surface of Chris's seeming spiritual rebellion, they didn't get rattled too much or too often.

As with all areas of adolescent development, teenagers will go through this transition in different ways and to varying degrees. That certainly has been the case in our own home. Some teens will continue to cruise along the path of spiritual growth without any prolonged doubts or questions. A few will reject the Christian faith and grasp another belief system. Others will dabble with different worldviews in order to submit Christianity to a comparison test. And still other teens will be like Chris: They'll act, question, and talk as though they've outgrown their childhood faith.

In his book *Like Dew Your Youth*, Eugene Peterson encourages parents to know that—

> His doubt and questioning and rebellion is evidence that something deeply significant is taking place in the personality of their offspring. Their teenagers are wondering what it is going to be like to maintain adult relationships with God. They are making the preparatory moves in coming to their adult, personal faith in Christ. It should be counted as a good time (if not a smooth time) because the parents can now share the struggles and achievements of their own Christian faith with these emerging persons. Resistance to the church is not the first step to atheism—it is more likely to be a natural development in discipleship.[35]

One of my teenagers went through a period of extended questioning that also included some poor choices, some rebellion, and a seeming disinterest in the faith of our family. We knew we couldn't drag this child into God's kingdom. We also knew God was working in ways we wouldn't always see or understand. In the end this child embraced our faith with increasing and *still* increasing sincerity and depth.

Our experience and the experience of others has shown that as a general (not hard-and-fast) rule, those teenagers whose parents have consistently taught and modeled the Christian faith will enter adulthood with a commitment to the faith they've been taught. And because they've gone through the difficult and sometimes painful process of personalizing their faith, their commitment is strong. It is theirs, and they are ready to live it and defend it! Others may continue on in the process for quite some time. We may not like or understand what's happening, but these are the times when God calls on us to be faithful and obedient followers of his Son while trusting in God's sovereignty, timing, and plan.

Whatever happened to Chris? Now in his early 40s, he's a youth worker. He has a special ability to communicate with kids whose age-related skepticism doesn't rattle him. He understands and offers them the same grace that he received. By loving them and answering their questions, Chris helps his students personalize and cement the valuable lessons they learned as children.

What You Can Do

The questioning attitude of a teenage child who's been

raised and instructed in the faith can be the most challenging and disheartening aspect of parenting for Christian parents. I know several who've weathered this storm and watched their children grow up with a faith that's become their own. In fact, many have embraced the storm knowing that in the long run their child will be better for having experienced it. When I ask parents how they got through it, they consistently offer these simple and valuable suggestions to parents who are still facing this challenge.

Be diligent in teaching young children by precept and example.

Talk about your faith. Spend time together learning to understand God's Word. Live and apply the Word to *all* areas of your life. And most important, allow your children the opportunity to see the fruit of that faith in your life. By doing so you'll help your children build a strong foundation.

Don't be upset when your children start to ask questions.

Rejecting the faith of your childhood is very different from asking honest questions and expressing doubt. Even if there is rejection, it may only be temporary. A teenager's struggle to find answers is a step on the road to spiritual growth. It's difficult to understand complicated theological issues; therefore, it's important to encourage their questions. The teenage years provide a good opportunity for parents to build relationships with their children by encouraging honest discussions about values, morals, and faith.

Encourage your teenager to be a vital part of your church.

A wise church family will seek to involve teenagers in a variety of leadership and service responsibilities. In addition, teens benefit from interaction with older Christians who, in the context of a loving relationship, freely share with vulnerability and honesty the godly wisdom that comes with advanced years and spiritual maturity. Keep in mind that this cannot happen if your church keeps the generations segregated during worship, education, fellowship, and service experiences.

Openly share your own doubts and struggles.

Today's teenagers value authenticity and vulnerability in parents and other adults. Let's face it—we are all sinful and fallen people whose lives have been marked by periods of struggle, doubt, problems, and failures. Sharing these with our children allows them to see us in our full humanity and dependence on God. In addition, it gives them permission not only to struggle and doubt, but also to openly share these struggles and doubts with their parents and other caring adults. Eugene Peterson writes, "If parents insist on keeping up a front of religious imperturbability, unflappable faith, and absolute assurance, all they will do is widen the credibility gap."[36]

Never, ever forget that spiritual growth is a process.

If you're a Christian parent, then your level of faith, spiritual maturity, and understanding isn't the same today as it was when you were a teenager. You've gone through a long process of growth that's still continuing. Don't expect your kids to be where you are in your faith. They're still in process, and they need time to grow. If we expect our kids to be at the point of full and faithful Christian maturity, then we may be facilitating their outward conformity to our expectations and standards—without having gone through real heart change and growth. Our desire should be for changed hearts that lead to a changed lifestyle. Outward conformity looks nice and can make us look good as parents, but it's only a front that will most likely come crashing down someday.

Remember that spiritual maturity is born out of struggle.

The Bible is filled with stories of rebellious human beings who were called by God to be his people but who often stubbornly followed their own will and way. While it would be wrong to excuse their sinful behavior, God always redeems horrible situations to bring his good out of our rebellious bad. I've watched lots of families struggle with kids who've wandered far from the family's faith, only to see those kids enter into adulthood with a deeper, more secure, and authentic faith. Maturity is born out of struggle.

Never stop praying for your kids.

We can never succeed in force-feeding faith to our kids. We can only teach them and answer their questions. The rest is in God's hands.

CHAPTER 8
Answers to Life's Big Questions

FOR OUR FIRST THREE YEARS OF MARRIAGE, MY wife and I lived just outside Boston. If you've ever had the opportunity to drive in or around Beantown, you know what I mean when I say that traffic regulations accepted by citizens in other parts of the country are sometimes totally disregarded there. With apologies to all my friends in Boston, I like to refer to this city's driving experience as "Darwinian" because you're surrounded by drivers who abide by only one rule of the road: *Survival of the fittest.*

Imagine coming from a relatively quiet and calm community and driving in Boston for the first time. I remember it well. People weren't stopping at stop signs. One-way streets went everywhere—but always in the wrong direction. You'd get in the inside lane of a traffic circle (or "rotary"), and the other drivers wouldn't let you out. Everyone drove offensively and horn honking abounded. The sudden changes in rules and driving environment shook me up. I never did get used to it. (Although my wife says I became one of those drivers!) I miss the city deeply, but I was happy to stop driving on the streets of Boston.

Adolescence isn't much different. A child cruises through the first 10 or 11 years of life only to arrive upon the streets of "Boston." The changes are confusing and overwhelming. Suddenly the rules are different. And if the physical, social, emotional, moral, and spiritual changes of adolescence aren't enough, there's more.

The rapid change and newness of adolescence is compounded by the fact that teenagers struggle to find answers to three life-shaping questions: *Who am I? Who are my friends?* and *Where am I going?* Thomas Hine says, "Despite the mythology of youth as a revolutionary and utopian time, study after study suggests that teenagers' principal preoccupation is to adapt, to find a place in life."[37] Curious and uncertain about life, teenagers are looking to make sense of the world and how they're to live in it. This wasn't an issue before humanity's fall into sin. But in our post-Genesis 3:6 world, everything is broken and flawed. Thus, all humanity asks the basic questions that are fundamental to life as a human being.

WHO AM I?

Without a doubt one of the most defining and single most important issues we must address in understanding and parenting adolescents is *identity formation*. The reason? It's the single most important developmental issue in a teenager's life. And the place they land now in terms of understanding themselves will in many ways determine who they are for the rest of their lives. In the end every teenager chooses to find her identity in something. And it's not just teenagers—it's the most important issue for all of us.

As I've worked with and raised teenagers, I've realized that this struggle to find oneself is normal, and it plays a role in determining who teenagers become as adults. Some developmental experts have labeled this process "the teenage identity crisis." Adolescents spend time trying to figure out who they are, and ultimately, who they will be for the rest of their lives. Most likely, you looked to certain identity models during your own teenage years: TV or music stars, sports icons, or people you knew. Your own sense about your changing self and lack of self-acceptance may have caused you to emulate your heroes and even try on some different "yous" for size and feel. Today's teenagers still dress, walk, talk, think, and act based on what they observe in the people they look up to. Thus, feelings of worthlessness and bouts of self-criticism will come and go as they evaluate where they are as compared to where they believe they should be.

In one way this adolescent search for identity isn't anything new. I grew up in the 1960s. I remember people stereotyping confused teenagers as being on a quest to "find themselves." Back then, the stereotype had the puzzled adolescent hopping into an old VW bus and heading to California on the quest to discover his identity. But the times have changed. Today, "California" comes to students 24/7 as the digital and media revolution has created a world where identity-shaping institutions and their messages live everywhere all the time.

In the quest to discover and adopt an identity, the teenagers you know and love are looking for answers to questions such as *Am I worthwhile? What makes me worthwhile? How am I unique? Is my uniqueness good or bad? What makes me special? And most importantly, Who am I?* In a perfect world, all teenagers would accept proper guidance and be drawn to godly, identity-shaping models. They'd understand themselves and find their identities in who they are as unique individuals created in the image of God for a relationship with him.

But we live in a fallen world that presents kids with two options: Finding one's identity in Christ, or choosing to find that identity in something else. Our kids embrace idolatry when they base their value, worth, and identity on someone or something other than God. Consequently we need to know who's sending them identity messages, what those messages are, and how kids are embracing those messages. To undo the wrong with the right, we must first know and understand the wrong that's being embraced and its nuances so we can challenge it with what's right and true.

The Search for Identity

Our imperfect world is marked by the waning influence of institutions (family and church) that traditionally helped teenagers understand and assume that their identity should be found *in* Christ. And as brokenness from our Creator continues to undo that perfect world and as those voices of truth grow dim, the door has been opened for other social factors and cultural institutions to step in and fill the void, sending powerful identity-shaping lessons that teach our kids who they should be and how they should live. Eventually, the blind start leading the blind, as equally young and confused influencers in the world of media and peers point the way through the teenaged years, telling our kids, "This is where you'll find your identity," and leaving them saying, "That's who I want to be."

So where are kids landing in their search for identity? And what effect is that having on their lives? In his book *The Reason for God*, Timothy Keller offers us answers that can shape the identity touchstones we look for and talk about with our kids. First, he defines *sin* in terms that speak volumes to the adolescent search for identity:

> Sin is not just the doing of bad things, but the making of good things into *ultimate* things. It is seeking to establish a sense of self by making something else more central to your significance, purpose, and happiness than your relationship to God.[38]

Then he goes on to share what he's learned as a culture watcher. While there are an infinite variety of "identity-bases," Keller's categories[39] sparked some thoughts and revisions of my own about the identity-bases that are living and thriving in today's youth culture.

Sexual partners and romantic others

With family breakdown on the rise, more and more teenagers are seeking intimacy and identity in their significant others or temporary sexual encounters. When our kids center their identities on their love or sexual interests, rather than on God, they'll become emotionally dependent, jealous, and controlling people. The other person's problems will become overwhelming to them. And they'll reduce the identity of others to pure objects.

Academic or athletic achievement

Many kids look for their value and worth in their accomplishments in the classroom or on the field. When this happens, they become driven, boring, and shallow. They can lose family and friends—unless their parents and friends are finding their own identities through these teenagers' successes. If something goes bad and it all falls apart—either temporarily or forever—then they consider themselves failures. Inevitably, the last whistle will blow or somebody else's grades will eclipse their own, and it will all come to an end. What then? Depression can set in. Might this offer a clue as to why so many kids today are depressed?

Money and possessions

Teenagers get hammered by marketing messages that leave them believing that "The one who dies with the most toys wins," "You are the brands you wear," and "You are what you own." Happiness is equated with having. But finding one's identity in stuff leads to being eaten up by worry and jealousy. In order to maintain and improve their lifestyle, they may choose to do unethical things. Eventually, life blows up. Like the rich young ruler, they walk away from Jesus very, very rich in the things of this world but unable to enjoy them because they're very, very sad.

Pleasure, gratification, and comfort

Our kids are growing up in a world in which pain is to be avoided at all costs while pleasure is something to be pursued. Kids want to "feel good." They take pills, abuse drugs, engage in extreme sports, binge drink, and get involved in all kinds of sexual behaviors to temporarily numb the pain and turn up the volume on the pleasure. The sad result, Tim Keller says, is that "you will find yourself getting addicted to something. You will become chained to the 'escape-strategies' by which you avoid the hardness of life."[40]

Relationships and approval

There's a scene in the film *Mean Girls* where the dastardly trio known as "The Plastics" stands in front of a single mirror, jockeying for position as each girl verbally criticizes her own flaws. What each one hopes is that the other two will argue away their self-criticism by denying the flaws exist. Kids who find their identity in relationships and peer approval will always be hurt by criticism and constantly lose their friends. Since they fear confrontation—both giving and getting—they wind up becoming useless friends.

Noble causes

The emerging generation of students wants to make a difference in the world. We know that more teenagers are getting involved in social causes today, and most of those causes are noble in character. But when one's identity is found in the cause and *not* in doing good as a servant of God who's committed to the cause of Christ, you begin to compartmentalize both people and the world into "good" and "bad." You demonize those who don't share your commitments. In the end you wind up being controlled by your enemies; and without them, your purpose fades.

Religion and morality

Today's teenagers are no more or less spiritual than previous generations. All humans since the beginning of time have been equally spiritual. The difference with today's kids is that their search is more *conscious* and *overt*. They're self-aware of their spirituality and deliberately embrace a variety of spiritual systems and beliefs. If this is where they find their identity, then they'll tend to be proud, self-righteous, and cruel when they're living up to their own moral standards. And when they aren't, they'll experience devastating guilt.

WHO ARE MY FRIENDS?

Did you know that according to the unwritten yet commonly understood rules of middle school life it's illegal for a girl to go to the restroom alone? The law requires that at least 12 girls travel together, even though only one of them has to go...or so you might think.

As children move into the early stages of adolescence, peers become increasingly important. One feels more secure when she's accepted by a group of friends, even if it's during a trip to the girls' restroom. An insecure and self-conscious teenager feels safe when hidden and accepted within the confines of a group.

When we ask teens what makes them feel "happiest" in life, one of the answers we consistently hear is this: "When I'm with my friends." Conversely, rejection is feared and oftentimes avoided at all costs. Many kids will impulsively and willingly compromise the standards of right and wrong if that compromise will keep them from standing out like a sore thumb and being rejected.

As teenagers move into high school and become more secure, the quantity of their friends usually decreases while the depth of their friendships increases. Teens may try on a number of different peer groups until they find their place. And changes in attitude, behavior, and dress may accompany their experimentation. While not always right, this tends to be "normal" behavior. Your kids are learning how to choose and develop friendships—a skill necessary for becoming a healthy adult and knowing how to choose adult friends, along with a lifelong marriage partner.

WHERE AM I GOING?

When I was young, I believed childhood would last forever and, like Peter Pan, I'd always be a boy. Then I became a teenager. As my high school years passed, people began asking me what I was going to do with my life, and I realized that I'd soon be responsible for myself. This was an important realization, as my parents had already made it clear that I wasn't going to live in their house forever.

One of the most awesome tasks of adolescence is making decisions about the future. As teenagers begin focusing on a vocational choice, they ask many questions: *What should I do with my life? How will I learn the necessary skills? Do I need to go to college? If so, where? What will I major in? How will I get a job? Will I get a job? Will I earn enough money? Where will I live? Will I get married?* The list goes on.

These questions can be difficult and overwhelming as teenagers cope with all of the other changes taking place. Yet, to become a responsible adult requires that these questions be answered. Parents must be sensitive to their teens as they face the task of searching out God's will and deciding what to do with their lives. Your gentle guidance, input, and direction are both valuable and valued.

What You Can Do

If our calling is ultimately about pointing kids to Christ and praying that he'd embrace them so hard that they'd find their identity solely in their embrace of him, then what can we do to help our kids find their way through youth culture's current muddled and confusing identity mess? Here are some suggestions to get you started.

Continually look in the mirror and ask yourself: *Where am I finding my identity?*

Tim Keller reminds us that "every person must find some way to 'justify their existence,' and to stave off the universal fear that they're a 'bum.'"[41] Ultimately, our identity can and must be found in Christ alone. We must be sure that with Augustine we are able to say, "Our hearts are restless until they find rest in Thee."

Continually observe the identity-shaping world.

Watching culture is not a once-and-done, past-tense activity. For the Christian parent, culture watching is an active, ongoing responsibility. Because culture is constantly shifting and changing, the responsibility lies with us to stay on top of the particularities and nuances of our kids' youth culture, particularly the messengers and messages that are shaping their identities. (You can learn more about youth culture in my book *Youth Culture 101*. And be sure to regularly visit our Center for Parent/Youth Understanding Web site—www. cpyu.org—as it's updated daily with information and analysis on today's youth culture.)

But it's not just something we do. It's something we do with a *purpose*. Theologian John Stott calls this "dual listening." He says we "stand between the Word and the world, with consequent obligation to listen to both. We listen to the Word in order to discover ever more of the riches of Christ. And we listen to the world in order to discover which of Christ's riches are needed most and how to present them in their best light."[42] When it comes to the task of shaping identity—both our own and our students'—dual listening is a necessity. We must know their world in order to bring the light of the Word to bear on it.

Continually confront the lies.

Several times during the Sermon on the Mount, Jesus issued "You have heard that it was said...but I tell you" statements. Each and every time, Jesus issued a corrective to conventional, widely held cultural wisdom that his hearers had not only heard, but had also allowed to become a part of their very lives. Jesus confronted and undid the cultural "you have heards" with his Word-centered "I tell yous."

As followers of Christ and ministers of his kingdom message, we need to follow suit. As already stated, first we must know the identity lies of our culture. Then we must shed the light of God's life-changing and identity-giving truth on those lies. A hallmark of our parenting is continually assuming the same "you have heard that it was said...but Jesus tells you" posture on identity matters.

Finally, nothing speaks louder than embodied truth. Adolescents are sharp—very sharp. It doesn't take long for them to pick up on what has a stranglehold on your identity. If you've embraced the Christ who has embraced you, then that mutual, life-giving stranglehold will serve as a compelling embodiment that turns conventional and cultural wisdom regarding where to find one's identity upside down! The *who* you are sends strong messages about the *who* they've been made to be.

History tells us that the famous monk Bernard of Clairvaux didn't always have his identity based in Christ. He was born into the luxury-filled life of nobility. But eventually he learned that his identity could only be found in Christ. And out of that experience of living on the foundation of a new identity-base, Bernard penned these words to his now-classic hymn: *Jesus, Thou joy of loving hearts! Thou fount of life, Thou light of men! From the best bliss that earth imparts, we turn unfilled to Thee again.* That, and only that, is the place where our kids will truly find themselves.

CHAPTER 9

Keep These Strategies in Mind

NOW THAT WE'VE COMPLETED OUR LOOK AT "normal" adolescent development, it's important to examine some time-tested strategies that will help us to maintain both a balanced personal perspective *and* a godly influence in our kids' lives as they pass through the teenage years. In no way, shape, or form do I claim to be an expert parent or an expert on parenting. I am a fellow struggler. But I've found that enlisting the following strategies (learned from my study of God's Word and the example of others who've gone before me in the journey of parenting teens) is important and necessary. The list is nowhere near exhaustive, but it's a good start to help teenagers live and grow through their adolescence, launching them into adulthood on a quest to love the Lord their God with all their hearts, souls, minds, and strength, and to love their neighbors as themselves.

BE ALL THAT YOU DESIRE THEM TO BE

In Deuteronomy 6, Moses shares God's plan for who was to

teach God's truths to succeeding generations and how they were to be taught:

> These commandments that I give you today are to be upon your hearts. Impress them on your children. Talk about them when you sit at home and when you walk along the road, when you lie down and when you get up. Tie them as symbols on your hands and bind them on your foreheads. Write them on the doorframes of your houses and on your gates. (Deuteronomy 6:6-9)

God's "who" are parents who have God's commandments written on their hearts and who gladly love God with their whole being. They are parents who prayerfully endeavor with God's help and by God's grace to integrate their faith into every nook and cranny of their lives. God, in his perfect wisdom and plan, has chosen to do his work through the family. God began with a family in Genesis, and God continues to use the family as the primary arena for bringing people to himself.

God's "how" for imparting these truths to our children is by a diligent commitment to teach and model wholehearted and single-minded devotion to God 24 hours a day. When God's truths become the central overriding interest and purpose in our lives, teaching them to our children will happen almost subconsciously.

It's no mistake that our children grow up to look, act, think, and be like us in so many ways. While similarities in physical appearance are inherited through the genes, our attitudes, values, and behaviors are passed from generation to generation by example. God designed it this way. This is especially true when it comes to faith development and spiritual health.

Here are some specific questions you can use to evaluate your own spiritual health and vitality. When my children look at me—

- Are they learning what it means to love God with all their hearts, souls, minds, and strength?
- Do they see me trusting God for guidance and wisdom as I plan the future, run my business, manage my home, and so on?
- Do they see me turning to God when I'm anxious, troubled, or ill?
- Do they see me living out my commitment to Christ by spending time reading and studying the Bible?
- Do they know that prayer is an important part of my life?
- Are they learning what it means to carry the cross and live a life of Christian discipleship?
- Do they see that God is central to my thoughts and actions constantly or just on Sunday mornings?
- Do they see a faith that is integrated into every area of my life, including my relationships, my vocation, my spending decisions, my use of leisure time, how I play, and so forth?
- Do they see me care for family, neighbors, friends, and the "lepers and outcasts" of the world?
- Are they learning to be compassionate and

Christ-centered, rather than insensitive and self-centered?
- Are they learning not to talk behind people's backs?
- Are they learning that God is the source of all they are and have, including the gift of salvation?

We all have wishes, dreams, hopes, and desires for what our children will become. When you dream about the spiritual future of your children, don't forget that they're learning what place spirituality and faith should hold in their lives— from you. Eugene Peterson describes it this way:

> A parent's main job is not to be a parent, but to be a person. There are no techniques to master that will make a good parent. There is no book to read that will give the right answers. The parent's main task is to be vulnerable in a living demonstration that adulthood is full, alive, and Christian.[43]

KNOW THEIR WORLD

If we're to live out our God-given calling to model and teach the Christian faith to our kids in a relevant manner, then we need to understand the cultural forces shaping the head and heart commitments of our kids. Only then can we teach them the value of using God's Word to navigate the challenges they'll face during their adolescent years and adulthood.

The coming years will bring more changes as the current youth culture continues to snowball away from your cultural experience of growing through your own teenage years. This means you'll have to be more intentional about keeping up. Read what your kids read. Listen to what they listen to. Watch what they watch. Continue on in the task you've begun because you need to know.

BE PROPHETIC

Those who've read and understand the Bible know that throughout the course of biblical history, God called certain people to speak his truth in his name. The Bible includes both a written record of the utterances of these prophets, along with several books of prophecy. When these divinely called and inspired prophets spoke, their words were the commands and revelations of God.

When I suggest that our approach to parenting our children be "prophetic," I'm certainly not suggesting that we take on the role of the religious cult leader who is a self-proclaimed prophet. Nor am I suggesting that we function in the way that Old and New Testament prophets functioned. Instead, being prophetic in our relationships with our teens is an intentional effort on our part to both know and communicate the truths of God's Word and how those truths speak to every area of their lives. In effect, it's the intentional process of looking for opportunities to speak biblical truth into their lives, showing how God's Word and the Christian faith speaks and relates to all of life. It's the process of imparting godly wisdom to our children and teenagers.

How do we do this? First and foremost, we should ask God to guide us in what, how, and when we communicate his truth. Unlike prophets of biblical times, this doesn't mean we wait for God's Spirit to move in our lives in a way that provokes an utterance or new revelation. Instead, we should ask God to guide us to the truths already spoken of in Scripture—along with how and when to communicate those truths to our kids.

Don't ever forget, there's no nook or cranny of our lives that lies outside of God's rule and reign. The Scriptures speak to every teenage pressure, choice, problem, or situation that's already been discussed in this book, along with a whole lot more. Part of our God-given responsibility is to communicate what God has said regarding these matters. In this way, we become prophetic in our parenting as we help our kids hear and understand God's revelation and commands.

BE PREVENTIVE

When our kids are little and first venture outside to play, we tell them to stay out of the street, to look both ways, and to keep away from strangers. We want them to be wise to the dangers that are out there so they'll avoid getting in harm's way. Parents who expect to lead their kids through adolescence and into spiritual health should also take preventive measures.

Our children and teenagers should be equipped to face life and all of its challenges. They need us to pass on the valuable information we've learned about life. We need to speak openly about the results of substance abuse, gluttony, premarital sex, pride, peer pressure, and materialism.

Another preventive measure is teaching our kids decision-making skills. There will come a time when they're out in the world without Mom or Dad at their side, and they'll be called upon to make some crucial choices. How will they know how to choose wisely if we haven't taken the time to tell them?

And they need parents who'll teach them the relevance of the truth of God's Word and how it applies to all of life. A working knowledge of God's transcendent standards of right and wrong is the best dose of preventive medicine. Your teen *will* face some very difficult pressures and choices during their teenage years...or perhaps even earlier. Your preventive influence must start now.

BE GRACE-FULLY REDEMPTIVE

How will you respond to your children when they make a mistake or do something wrong? What will you say if your daughter turns her back on all that you taught her and becomes sexually active—and pregnant? What will you say if your son gets suspended from school for fighting? What will you do if you find drug paraphernalia in your teenager's room? What will you do if your daughter gets arrested for shoplifting? Remember that just like you and me, your teens' sinfulness is the greatest problem they face. *All* teenagers will encounter temptation, and *all* teenagers will make sinful choices. The determining factor in whether a bad choice turns into a situation that gets better or worse is your response.

Let me suggest that your goal should be to redeem these situations by turning a mistake into an opportunity for your teenager to become a more godly and Christlike person. Don't write off your teenager as hopeless or boot him out of the family. Rather, treat him as you believe your heavenly Father would treat you if you were the offending party—because there isn't a day that goes by that you aren't. Believe me, I know.

> Paul Tripp reminds us:
> We need to face the fact that the harsh realities of the Fall are depicted in everyday family life. It is this humble admission that opens us up to one of the greatest functions of the Christian family. It is when we humbly face the reality of our falseness that we begin to seek and treasure the riches of the grace of the Lord Jesus Christ. As we—parents and children alike—face our need as sinners, the family becomes a truly redemptive community where the themes of grace, forgiveness, deliverance from sin, reconciliation, new life in Christ, and hope become the central themes of family life.[44]

John Seel writes, "So what is Christian parenting? In short, it's loving our children as God loves us. It's emulating the father of the prodigal son who loved him enough to let him leave and squander his inheritance."[45]

One of the unforgettable lessons I remember hearing from Dr. John White was in response to a question he was asked about how he'd learned to relate to his own wayward son. White simply said he'd learned to live his life according to this simple yet profound principle: "As Christ is to me, so must I be to my children."

My heavenly father has showered me with tremendous amounts of love and amazing grace. Along with the apostle Paul, I have to say, "But God demonstrates his own love for us in this: While we were still sinners, Christ died for us" (Romans 5:8), and "The grace of our Lord was poured out on me abundantly, along with the faith and love that are in Christ Jesus. Here is a trustworthy saying that deserves full acceptance: Christ Jesus came into the world to save sinners—of whom I am the worst" (1 Timothy 1:14-15). I've been the recipient of abundant grace.

Why, then, have I been far less than graceful with my own kids so many times? When they fail miserably or do something wrong, I'm usually quick to jump down their throats, condemning both them and their sin. But then I'm reminded of what Christ has done for me in his mercy and grace, and I'm put to shame.

When mistakes, difficulty, and rebellion rear their ugly heads in your home—and they will—remember how your heavenly Father has treated you. If you're like me, then nothing your kids can do or say comes even close to your daily and habitual rebellion against God.

BE NOT AFRAID

Parenting teenagers can be scary. I even had one adult tell me that watching kids go through the teenage years is the most effective birth-control method around. Yes, the teenage years are difficult for both kids and their parents. But should we be afraid?

While parents should be cautious, watchful, and discerning, we cannot allow ourselves to fall victim to fear. Usually this fear either manifests itself in a desire to remove our kids from the world and thereby keep them from harm, or it immobilizes us as parents, keeping us from fulfilling our God-given role in our teenagers' lives.

God's dealings with people, as recounted in the Scriptures, reveal the attitude we should have regarding the latter immobilizing manifestation of fear. John Stott sums it up this way:

> All fear brings a measure of paralysis. Nobody who is afraid is free. Moreover, fear is like fungus: it grows most rapidly in the dark. It is essential, therefore, to bring our fears out into the light and look at them, especially in the light of the victory and supremacy of Jesus Christ. For he who died and rose has also been exalted to his Father's right hand, and everything has been put under his feet. So where are the things of which we were previously afraid? They are under the feet of the triumphant Christ. It is when we see them there that their power to terrify is broken.[46]

As a parent of teenagers, I've learned that the comforting words that the angel of the Lord spoke to the shepherds keeping watch over their flocks at night also apply to me. To be honest, I wrestle to accept them from time to time. But still, I'm told: Do not be afraid.

YOU HAVE A LAMP—USE IT

In many ways life is a mysterious journey. I've been on mine for more than 50 years now. And just when I begin to discover the answers to my questions, I enter a new phase of the journey with its own set of confusing choices and circumstances. The questions keep coming. The confusion always seems to be there. Whether we're children, teenagers, or adults, we all look to some authority for answers. That authority—be it a friend, parent, spouse, writer, film star, musician, ourselves, or even our changing opinions—becomes our guiding light, directing our steps as we try to figure out where we're from, where we belong, and how to get there.

In a world in which there are many "experts" sharing conflicting opinions on the purpose of life, how to live our lives, and how to raise and relate to kids, it's good to know there's a light we can trust. And the One who created life, children, teenagers, parents, and families is handing it to us. That light is the Word—both the incarnate Word Jesus Christ and the written Word. Together, the example of Christ and God's revelation of himself in the Bible reveals what we need to know about everything we encounter on the journey.

Keep the Dust Off the Good Book

The words that the apostle Paul wrote to Timothy, a young man who needed encouragement, also apply to us today as we fulfill our God-given ministry in parenting or ministering to kids: "Every part of Scripture is God-breathed and useful one way or another—showing us truth, exposing our rebellion, correcting our mistakes, training us to live God's way" (2 Timothy 3:16, MSG). In this verse, Paul lists four valuable purposes the light serves:

1. **The Bible offers sound instruction.** It's a believable teacher and the only true source of knowledge about God's world. Like the instruction manual accompanying a complicated machine or appliance, God's Word helps us to understand and bear the complexities of life, including our changing children and their confusing world.

2. **A growing knowledge of the Bible helps us evaluate and test everything else that claims to be true.** All worldviews, parenting philosophies, advice, manuals, and approaches should be measured against the blueprint of the Bible.

3. **The Bible can serve as a diagnostic checkup and troubleshooting guide.** As we look at our own lives and approaches to parenting, the Bible helps us see where we've gone wrong, while offering clear guidelines and instruction on how to correct our course.

4. **The Bible is a road map that helps us stay on course in all of our tasks and activities.** It lays out a clear path for right and godly living. In a day and age when some kids grow up without parents or any other positive role models, our children and teenagers desperately need godly parents and youth leaders whose disciplined and

regular study of and meditation on Scripture pays liberal dividends in Christlike love and direction.

BE PRAYERFUL

Parents, we need to pray for answers—answers to our questions about raising children and answers to our adolescents' questions and their deep spiritual longing for God. You see, our children grow in the wisdom and nurture of God in spite of us, not because of us. Sure, they learn a lot from the example we live, but the fact of the matter is that it's ultimately God who gives faith to our kids and leads them to spiritual health.

Paul's words became more real to me as I struggled to raise my kids through adolescence: "Do not be anxious about anything, but in everything, by prayer and petition, with thanksgiving, present your requests to God" (Philippians 4:6). Prayer is God's gift to us as we depend on him and his power to keep us on track as moms and dads.

CHAPTER 10
Getting Personal

IT WOULD BE MUCH EASIER FOR PARENTS IF there were a universal adolescent experience. And if this were the case, then someone would have come up with a formula for success long ago, and we'd all be experts at understanding and parenting adolescents. But because each child responds uniquely to the challenges of change, parents will have plenty of surprises. The interdependency between all of the developmental areas simply means that changes in one area will cause changes in the others. For example, a child's slow physical development may cause social stress and rejection that could lead to either a deepened faith in God or to an animosity toward a God whom she believes has ruined her life.

When asked what was so tough about becoming an adult, a 16-year-old said this: "Everything about being a teenager is hard. I just don't want to go through it alone. My greatest fear is that I'll wake up some morning and be a nobody." As parents, we need to put ourselves in our teenagers' shoes and remember our own adolescence. Although times have changed, the changes and associated feelings kids experience have not. Think back to your teenage years—to the painful times, the joyous times, the day you were teased. How did you feel?

I remember the time in seventh grade when all the guys in my class were jealous because I was assigned a homeroom seat next to a well-developed girl named Sherri. Out of the 200 girls in seventh grade, she looked the most like a woman. Then one day she was gone, and I never saw her again. It turns out she'd left school to have a baby—a confusing thing that was hard for my young mind to comprehend or understand.

I also remember walking between classes and thinking that every eye was on me and my perceived imperfections. I remember how time seemed to stand still in math class. I tried as hard as I could to understand math, but I just couldn't get it. I felt like a failure. Then there was gym class, during which the physical abilities of the haves and the have-nots were accentuated and revealed for all to see. And in the locker room, our physical attributes were made visible to all. Even though we were the same age, a glance around the community shower proved that we were all developing at different rates. Some looked like my dad. Others, like my little brother. I wondered what my peers saw when they looked at me.

As Cliff Schimmels has said, adolescence is "a time of transition for both the child and the parent. The child has to learn to handle changing roles, moods, and body. You as parents have to learn to handle the changing child."[47]

I clearly remember the first time the dark side of adolescence reared its ugly head in our home. I approached our then-12-year-old daughter Caitlin to offer correction and discipline for a lapse in judgment. But the little girl who'd always listened and responded with repentance put up a fight. I found myself feeling somewhat numb, as I was a rookie at this sort of thing. When our encounter quickly escalated, I decided to put an end to it by sending her to her room. She stomped up the steps, went into her room, and slammed the door. The stomping and the slamming sent me over the edge. So I stomped up the steps after her, and then I let her have it as I verbally unloaded my anger on her.

After leaving Caitlin's room, I went to my own room and sat down to cool off. Then my wife calmly intervened and said to me, "Don't you ever listen to what you tell all those parents? You need to remember that she's at a point where she's not even sure what's going on in her life."

When we'd both cooled down, Caitlin was more forgiving than I was. She even took a part of her punishment surprisingly well—having the door to her room removed for a week. While we can't excuse rebellious behavior, we do need to understand our teenagers better than they understand themselves. That's a lesson I learned that day.

If you let them, teenagers can get under your skin and drive you crazy. If you understand them—and the changes taking place in their lives that they don't even understand—then you can fulfill your God-given responsibility. You can help them survive the earthquake of adolescence that strikes between childhood and a healthy, productive adult life in which they enthusiastically embrace the Jesus who has embraced them and seek to glorify him through all they are, all they have, and all they do.

May the God who is parenting you bless you as you parent your teenager. And may God make you a blessing to your kids.

FOR FURTHER READING

The following lists include some of the books I've written, along with titles that I've found to be especially helpful as I've endeavored to understand teenagers and the period of life known as adolescence. These lists aren't exhaustive, but they're a good start.

Writings of Walt Mueller
Engaging the Soul of Youth Culture: Bridging Teen Worldviews and Christian Truth (InterVarsity Press, 2006). A practical guide to teen worldviews, along with a helpful paradigm you can use to engage your teenagers in discussions about matters of faith and life.

I Want to Talk with My Teen about Movies, Music and More (Standard, 2006). A practical guide for parents who want to understand and influence their teenagers' media choices.

Opie Doesn't Live Here Anymore: Where Faith, Family, and Culture Collide (Standard, 2007). A collection of my blogs and articles that wrestle with the connection between Christian faith and the cultural issues our kids face on a daily basis.

Youth Culture 101 (Zondervan/Youth Specialties, 2007). Offers an overview of the cultural soup our kids swim in every day.

Recommended Reading on Adolescent Issues
Chap Clark, *Hurt: Inside the World of Today's Teenagers* (Baker, 2004). Offers deep insights into the state of adolescence in contemporary America. A great book for strengthening your understanding of your teenager and motivating you to actively respond through relationships.

Steve Gerali, *Teenage Guys: Exploring Issues Adolescent Guys Face and Strategies to Help Them* (Zondervan/Youth Specialties, 2006). Provides a deep and practical look into adolescent male development in today's world.

Joe S. McIlhaney, Jr. and Freda McKissic Bush, Hooked: New Science on How Casual Sex Is Affecting Our Children (Northfield, 2008). Offers compelling scientific findings on adolescent brain development, sexuality, and relationships.

Ginny Olson, *Teenage Girls: Exploring Issues Adolescent Girls Face and Strategies to Help Them* (Zondervan/Youth Specialties, 2006). Provides a deep and practical look into female adolescent development in today's world.

Donald Opitz and Derek Melleby, *The Outrageous Idea of Academic Faithfulness: A Guide for Students* (Brazos, 2007). Are your teenagers planning to attend college? This is a great book that helps late adolescents prepare for college life in a way that brings honor and glory to God.

John Piper, *Don't Waste Your Life* (Crossway, 2003). Provides a wonderful challenge to teenagers and young adults about integrating their Christian faith into all of life as they launch from adolescence into adulthood.

Recommended Reading on Parenting Adolescents
Ken R. Canfield, *The Seven Secrets of Effective Fathers: Becoming the Father Your Children Need* (Tyndale House, 1992). A book that every father should read.

Steve Dunn, *Bored with God: How Parents, Youth Leaders and Teachers Can Overcome Student Apathy* (InterVarsity, 2004). The title is self-explanatory. A great book to encourage you as your encourage your teenager's spiritual growth and development.

J. Thomas Fitch and Melissa R. Cox, eds., *Questions Kids Ask about Sex: Honest Answers for Every Age* (Revell, 2005). From the physicians at The Medical Institute for Sexual Health, this helpful guide offers faith-based and scientifically accurate answers to all the questions kids have about their developing sexuality.

C. John Miller and Barbara Miller Juliani, *Come Back, Barbara* (P&R Publishing, 1997). A real-life story of hope and redemption for those struggling to make sense of their relationships with their prodigal teens.

Les Parrot III, *Helping Your Struggling Teenager: A Parenting Handbook on Thirty-Six Common Problems* (Zondervan, 2000). Categorized for easy and quick reference, this guide to difficult issues teenagers face offers valuable explanations, insight into dynamics, and practical step-by-step responses.

Marv Penner, *Help! My Kids Are Hurting: A Survival Guide to Working with Students in Pain* (Zondervan/Youth Specialties, 2005). An adolescent counselor and youth ministry expert offers insight and advice on how to handle the major crisis issues kids face during their teenage years.

Wayne Rice, ed., *There's a Teenager in My House: 101 Questions Parents Ask* (InterVarsity, 2005). Wayne Rice and a host of experts on adolescence provide helpful and practical answers to the most common questions parents have about raising and relating to teens.

Paul David Tripp, *Age of Opportunity: A Biblical Guide to Parenting Teens* (P&R Publishing, 2001). Practical, realistic, and vulnerable. This is hands-down the best parenting book I've ever read.

Rich Van Pelt and Jim Hancock, *A Parent's Guide to Helping Teenagers in Crisis* (Zondervan/Youth Specialties, 2007). Two seasoned adolescent-crisis experts walk parents through redemptive responses to adolescent crises.

John White, *Parents in Pain: Overcoming the Hurt and Frustration of Problem Children* (InterVarsity, 1979). A great book on responding redemptively to difficult times with your teenagers.

NOTES

1. Jody W. Zylke, "Characterizing Healthy Adolescent Development; Distinguishing It from Possible Disturbances," *Journal of the American Medical Association* 262, no. 7 (August 1989): 880.

2. Anne Lamott, *Grace (Eventually): Thoughts on Faith* (New York: Riverhead Books, 2007), 183.

3. Chap Clark, *Hurt: Inside the World of Today's Teenagers* (Grand Rapids, MI: Baker Academic, 2004), 27.

4. Eugene Peterson, *Like Dew Your Youth: Growing Up with Your Teenager* (Grand Rapids, MI: Eerdmans, 1998), 1.

5. To learn more about how teenagers and adolescence developed in the United States during the 20th century, see Thomas Hine, *The Rise and Fall of the American Teenager* (New York: Avon Books, 1999).

6. Paul David Tripp, *Age of Opportunity: A Biblical Guide to Parenting Teens* (Phillipsburg, NJ: P&R Publishing, 2001), 19-20.

7. Lamott, *Grace (Eventually)*, 193-4.

8. Dean Borgman, *When Kumbaya Is Not Enough: A Practical Theology for Youth Ministry* (Peabody, MA: Hendrickson, 1997), 116.

9. Peterson, *Like Dew Your Youth*, 2.

10. C. John Miller and Barbara Miller Juliani, *Come Back, Barbara*, 2nd ed. (Phillipsburg, NJ: P&R Publishing, 1997), 165.

11. John Foxe, *Christ Jesus Triumphant*, quoted in Bernard Bangley, *Near to the Heart of God: Daily Readings from the Spiritual Classics* (Wheaton, IL: Harold Shaw Publishers, 1998), 112.

12. Michael Card, *The Hidden Face of God: Finding the Missing Door to the Father Through Lament* (Colorado Springs, CO: NavPress, 2007), 46.

13. Alistar McGrath, *The Unknown God: Searching for Spiritual Fulfillment* (Grand Rapids, MI: Eerdmans, 1999), 120.

14. John Stott, *The Contemporary Christian: Applying God's Word to Today's World* (Downers Grove, IL: InterVarsity, 1992), 39.

15. Earl D. Wilson, *You Try Being a Teenager!* (Portland, OR: Multnomah Press, 1982), 21-2.

16. Peter Zollo, *Getting Wiser to Teens: More Insights into Marketing to Teenagers* (Ithaca, NY: New Strategist, 2004), 36.

17. Lamott, *Grace (Eventually)*, 189-90.

18. David Walsh, *WHY Do They Act That Way?* (New York: Free Press, 2004), 1.

19. Ibid., 15.

20. Tripp, *Age of Opportunity*, 13ff.

21. Ibid., 19-20.

22. Walsh, *WHY Do They Act That Way?*, 15.

23. Thomas Hine, *The Rise and Fall of the American Teenager* (New York: Avon Books, 1999), 31.

24. *The State of our Nation's Youth: 2005-2006* (Alexandria, VA: The Horatio Alger Association of Distinguished Americans, 2005), 32-3.

25. Zollo, *Getting Wiser to Teens*, 46.

26. Dale A. Blyth and Carol Traeger, "Adolescent Self-Esteem and Perceived Relationships with Parents and Peers," *Social Networks of Children, Adolescents, and College Students*, ed. Suzanne Salzinger, John Antrobus, and Muriel Hammer (Hillsdale, NJ: Lawrence Erlbaum Associates, 1988), 188; and Patricia Clark Blake and John R. Slate, "A Preliminary Investigation into the Relationship Between Adolescent Self-Esteem and Parental Verbal Interaction," *School Counselor* 41, no. 2 (November 1993): 81ff.

27. Walsh, *WHY Do They Act That Way?*, 236.

28. Claudia Wallis, Alice Park, and Kristina Dell, "What Makes Teens Tick," *Time* (May 10, 2004), 56-65.

29. Joe S. McIlhaney, Jr. and Freda McKissic Bush, *Hooked: New Science on How Casual Sex Is Affecting Our Children* (Chicago: Northfield Publishing, 2008), 55-6.

30. Ibid., 56.

31. Ibid., 52.

32. Ravi Zacharias, "An Ancient Message, Through Modern Means, to a Postmodern Mind," in *Telling the Truth*, ed. D.A. Carson (Grand Rapids, MI: Zondervan, 2000), 26.

33. Peterson, *Like Dew Your Youth*, 90.

34. Clark, *Hurt*, 189.

35. Peterson, *Like Dew Your Youth*, 27.

36. Ibid., 24.

37. Hine, *The Rise and Fall of the American Teenager*, 2.

38. Timothy Keller, *The Reason for God: Belief in an Age of Skepticism* (New York: Dutton, 2008), 162.

39. Ibid., 275-76.

40. Ibid.

41. Ibid., 164.

42. Stott, *The Contemporary Christian: Applying God's Word to Today's World*, 110-11.

43. Peterson, *Like Dew Your Youth*, 10.

44. Tripp, *Age of Opportunity*, 66.

45. David John Seel, Jr., *Parenting Without Perfection: Being a Kingdom Influence in a Toxic World* (Colorado Springs, CO: Navpress, 2000), 37.

46. Stott, *The Contemporary Christian*, 51.

47. Cliff Schimmels, *What Parents Try to Forget About Adolescence* (Elgin, IL: David C. Cook, 1989), 179.

The Center for Parent/Youth Understanding exists to help you understand, raise, and relate to your children and teens. For a host of helpful resources and information on teenagers and their world that's updated daily, please visit us at **www.cpyu.org**.